A stirring and brilliant call to action for everyone invested in the well-being of young people—educators, parents, and KidLit writers alike. Qarooni provides a framework for how we can better exalt young people in all of their complexity, braiding together their lived experiences from school to home and everything in between. This book gave me so much to think about as both a parent and as a writer and advocate for young people.

—Jasmine Warga
Author of *A Rover's Story and Other Words for Home*

Through a series of deeply personal family stories intertwined with practical tools for reflection and action, Nawal Qarooni challenges educators to recast our conceptions of family literacy engagement and brings to life what truly centering family, community, and relationships can mean for supporting students' pursuit of advanced literacy.

—Jane Fleming
Coauthor of *More Mirrors in the Classroom:*
*Using Urban Children's Literature to Increase Literacy*

This book is both brilliant and artful. Its content, its narrative, and even its gorgeous design bring forward a generous and care-full vision of the relationships between literacy and love, kinship and learning, school and home. What an absolutely stunning treasure.

—Carla Shalaby
Author of *Troublemakers: Lessons in Freedom from Young Children at School*

*Nourishing Caregiver Collaborations* provides a fresh and humanistic perspective into how educators can engage with caregivers in authentic and dynamic ways. This book will warm your educator soul with its beautiful stories and message, inspire you to rethink and reimagine family engagement, and provide practical next steps for application.

—Dr. Cindy Bak
Assistant Director at the Cotsen Foundation for the ART of TEACHING

# Nourishing Caregiver Collaborations

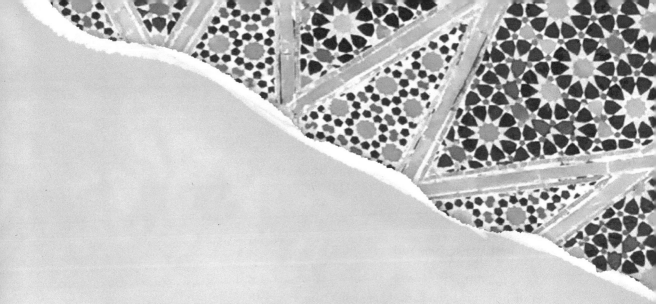

# Nourishing Caregiver Collaborations:

## Exalting Home Experiences and Classroom Practices for Collective Care

### Nawal Qarooni

Foreword by Cornelius Minor

 Routledge
Taylor & Francis Group

NEW YORK AND LONDON

A Stenhouse Book

Cover design by Cindy Butler and Sahar Ghaheri
Interior design by Sahar Ghaheri and Jill Shaffer

First published 2024
by Routledge
605 Third Avenue, New York, NY 10158

and by Routledge
4 Park Square, Milton Park, Abingdon, Oxon, OX14 4RN

*Routledge is an imprint of the Taylor & Francis Group, an informa business*

© 2024 Nawal Qarooni

ISBN: 9781625316196 (pbk)
ISBN: 9781032681917 (ebk)

DOI: 10.4324/9781032681917

Typeset in Baskerville URW
by Eclipse Publishing Services

For my parents: Kamal and Mahnaz

*I am because you are.*


For my children: Eliana Noor, Ehsan Noel,
Ezzat Naya, and Eloisa Nasim

*Be like water. Flow unapologetically.*


we are each other's
harvest:
we are each other's
business:
we are each other's
magnitude and bond

~Gwendolyn Brooks

# Contents

# A Note to the Reader

Writing a book is an immensely humbling, community act—an experience made possible by the people who loved and cared for me and my children while I wrote, grew ideas alongside me, and kept laughter in my life.

This book is a moment in time for my thinking and practice, an offering of what I've learned. I want to acknowledge too that people grow and change, just as language does, so my thinking (and maybe even the terminology in this book) will be ever evolving. When I was a newspaper reporter, I would crank out breaking news stories that literally went in the trash the next day. There was no revising. It is difficult to call a book "done" when its very essence centers a plea for its readers to perpetually remix. In my work, I seek to ask questions and open a conversation, to provide pathways rather than one-way answers.

The idea for this manuscript sprung from the COVID-19 pandemic, when I had four babies to care for at home while supporting teachers in dozens of Chicago schools virtually. I nursed my baby under the Zoom screen for two years. While juggling cooking and cleaning and working and mothering, I realized what caregivers all over the world had been doing for centuries—collective care. Growing literate thinkers, no matter what setting. I also realized how little we understood of each other's "work" until the pandemic forced us to really look.

In *Essential Labor: Mothering as Social Change*, Angela Garbes writes, "The terrain of mothering is not limited to the people who give birth to children; it is not defined by gender . . . it is the action of mothering, which includes anyone who is engaged in 'the practice of creating, nurturing, affirming and supporting life'" (2022). In writing this book, I wanted to exalt all the actions I saw, both in classrooms and in homes, to expand this spirit of mothering to the contributions caregivers and communities make every day. I saw how the authentic reciprocity in these relationships between home and school can breathe life into how we can embrace teaching and learning too.

This book is a journey of transition. While my ideas formed, my kids grew leggy and long. It's a very Chicago and Jersey City book: a book that straddles where I lived and worked for the last fifteen years. I lost two of my closest relatives—two of the most unapologetic and alive—while I wrote. I grieved openly. I transitioned this manuscript from one publisher to another. I reimagined what work and home could look like. I turned forty.

I am blessed with an incredible collective: people I've learned from and leaned on as I've been in process, people who know that sister and mother are verbs.

Terry Thompson: you dear human, you. What a *joy* it has been to shepherd this book into the world with you as my guide. You understood my work habits, my priorities, my family needs, and my voice—early—and advocated for my preferences every step of the way.

To Zoë Ryder White: thank you for cheering me on when my caregiver literacy ideas were in infancy. To the Big Shoulders team: Liz Bartley, Eliza Bryant, Stacy Ginnochio, Rebecca Ryan, and Kristin Ziemke, you all are dream collaborators. Marv Hoffman: thank you for being the ultimate connector and fountain of wisdom. To Jane Fleming and the CPS Department of Literacy team: your vision for the future of Chicago children is one we are proud to fight for. To the Cotsen Foundation team: Angela Bae, Cindy Bak, and Julie Graham, your positivity and love for the art of teaching is truly refreshing; way to *take care* of the collective. Thank you all for providing such a gorgeous home for my family literacy ideas and for cultivating space for teachers to extend their excitement into everyday practice.

**To the students and families** I've worked with in my residencies, to everyone who welcomed a traveling teacher with smiles and hugs: thank you. To the children of Brooklyn, where I started my career: I love you with everything inside of me. *You make me feel alive.* To my building principals, I appreciate you and your relentless dedication. To the Ramos family: thank you for sharing your love with us.

**To my team at NQC Literacy:** Elana Porat and Sarah Skoda, it's impossible to explain what pride and comfort you bring me daily, making a real and lasting difference with your nourishing practices and loving mama-literacy-coach lenses. Thank you for rooting for me. Thank you for doing more than I ask before I even articulate the need myself. And thank you for reminding me what's important.

Cornelius: thank you for believing in me. Jaclyn Karabinas: thank you for your detail-oriented eye and loving me so hard across the finish line. Kate Roberts: I appreciate your literacy and life mentoring, both. Tiffany Jewel: you lovingly practice what you preach. My mama scholars, Luz Yadira Herrera, Carla España, Jasmine Warga: thank you for keeping it real, always inspiring me, *and* allowing me to just *be*. You three are a gift.

My dear Ryan(s): the epitome of love and acceptance. To my high school friends: for the beautiful mess that shaped us. Chris-Annmarie and Acasia: for sustaining sacred adult friendships. David and Zamira: for caring for my children as your own. Tony and Angela: your unwavering support means the world. Kate and Sarah: blueprint for listening and compassion, unparalleled. How you show up slays me. Dear gorgeous humans I'm lucky enough to be close to, your belly-deep laugh tracks are life giving. My first babies: Rami and Dali, coraising you offered initial gifts in mothering. Always proud of you. Sahary: there's never a day that I'm not grateful we're in it together. To the Casiano and Crehore clans: love you all so very much.

**To my own caregiving collective:** Rezy, Hossy, Afi, Uncle Nezam, Rikke. Ameh Shamsi, Uncle Hamid. Neda e aziz. Khalehaye Shiraz. My grandparents, my ancestors, who move through me still. My parents, the people who made me. You've taught me more about resilience, strength, and what matters—beyond any book. Jon: Thank you for building this life with me. *I love all of this.* To the babies I gave birth to and grew. My own flesh and blood: it is not enough to say "love" in Arabic. You must say "be the thing that buries me."\* *You are.*

\*After my dear Hala Alyan, *Interactive :: House Saints 2020*

## Design Note:

The cover, chapter openers, and various design elements in this book were created by Sahar Ghaheri, my closest cousin. All of the images layered into the design are our family photos or were taken by one of us. They reflect a Middle Eastern tradition and the idea that peeling back the layers of one's identity reveals an authentic, literacy-rich lineage that includes place, people, food, and story. The photographs are not representative of the wide-ranging ancestries of all readers, but it is our hope that my family experiences can be transferred to our understanding of students and their expansive histories.                    —NQ

# Foreword

School has never existed in isolation. It is tied to community. What happens at school—from learning to relationships—is a byproduct of what happens in front yards and back seats. School is linked to economics. Influenced by policy. Impacted by culture. But it is informed by home.

Nawal Qarooni knows home.

And though home is different to all of us, she knows that you know it too.

And we know that home isn't simply a house or an apartment . . . or a shelter or a settlement. Home is where the people who shape our growth can be found. These people—caregivers—are the parents, relatives, and community members to whom we are bonded by blood, by choice, or by circumstance.

These are the folks that stand by us. And the lessons that we were made to learn in the vacuum of their absences.

These are the folks that carry us. And the insights we gained from the times when they couldn't.

These are the folks that love us. And the fortitude that we have forged from becoming beings who can love ourselves.

Our homes: Perfectly imperfect. Human.

Nawal knows this humanity. She parents with it. She teaches with it. She writes with it. She lives it.

We are teaching in a historical moment defined by fear.

We have survived a pandemic, watched democracies erode, economies recede, and rights evaporate.

Our communities are reeling from this . . . or pretending that it isn't happening.

Our children are hurting from this . . . or their futures are hurting from the knowledge and the critical thinking that is being denied them by those who misguidedly want to "protect" them.

Fear has compelled some among us to opine, "school should just be school"—a place where children leave the world outside, and learners come inside for simple reading and writing.

What Nawal knows, and what she shares here, is that if kids leave the world outside, they leave their humanity with it. So much of what is in the world is in them.

So much of what is right about the world exists because of what is right with their caregivers and families.

This book is a guide for how to strengthen our teaching with the vitality of our families. It is about how to invite caregivers in; when so much of modern adulting is pushing them away—away from their children, away from school, away from each other, and away from the experience of being themselves.

This book is a prescription for how to hold our communities together at a time when there is so much that threatens to tear them asunder.

This book is a beacon to everyone who is looking for the light. Recent history has taught us that there is little light to be found in gilded policy or sanitized curriculum or shiny programs served to us by politicians and gurus. These things have let us down before.

Here, Nawal provides necessary redirection for our profession. She reminds us that illumination lives at home—in every recipe, in every ritual, and in every relative. And she shows us how to connect those things to the learning that happens at school.

When mothers sing to their children, that is literacy.

When uncles debate cousins in barber shops, that is literacy.

When neighbors compare movie previews to decide what to watch, that is literacy.

When families grow vegetables, go fishing, do yard work, pay bills, play games, or drive home in the evening; all of these are rich opportunities to observe the world, think, form ideas, and build knowledge. The way that children do these things at home can inform how we strengthen those skills in school.

All children come to us with a universe of experiences and insight that they have grown alongside their caregivers. The work that families have done in the home is organic, yes. This does not mean that it is not academic.

Bathing a sibling while a grandparent prepares the meal is as challenging and as rigorous as anything that a student might invest in at school. We can be the ones that help them to see the genius in what they already do. The executive skill, rhetorical power, creativity, reflection, and organization required to live are the same skills and habits of mind required to be fully literate in our society. And we can help kids to do the kind of translation—transference—to see how the practice of being fluently human at home has equipped them perfectly as they learn to be fluently literate at school.

Here, Nawal advocates for new ways of seeing what we see every day. She leads us to see home rituals not as separate from school, but as a compliment to school. That we see our own histories and humanity not as separate from the work that we do as educators, but as an essential part of it.

In this ecosystem of fear, hers is an intrepid, necessary, and loving voice.

So is yours.

This book is a manual for how to use your voice, as she does: in concert with communities of caregivers, to stitch our world and our work back together. One beautiful family at a time.

Cornelius Minor
Parent, educator, dedicated fan of Nawal
Brooklyn, New York

# Kilim as a Pedagogical Stance

The tradition of kilim making in the Middle East extends back thousands of years. My family has revered this ancient rug-weaving art for as long as I can remember. For some, home is where the sounds of their loved ones echo off the walls. For others, home is where the aroma of their traditional spices fills the air: garlic, onion, and turmeric, or ginger, mint, and lemongrass. For me, these experiences are true in addition to the presence of kilim rugs beneath our feet, brought from Iran or Turkey or Afghanistan, along with their stories.

Throughout this book, you'll see references to kilim as metaphor. To me, these patterned beauties represent intentionality and uniqueness as well as durability, intricacy, and intimacy. No two kilims are alike. Often, they are hand-dyed with vegetable-based colors, drawing from Mother Earth and her natural abundance. Each Kilim rug tells the story of the weaver who made it—sometimes with familiar animals and objects; sometimes as an actual message to a loved one. They are organized with geometric principles but often reveal unexpected beauty in their asymmetrical or irregular patterns. And that's what's so perfect about them.

They are nuanced. They are varied. They are meaningful. And when we handle them with care, treating them with respect in our homes across the years, they come to embody a collective, unified whole that speaks to a shared value, culture, and history. Once we exalt the kilim—simultaneously awe-inspiring and comforting in its simple consistency—to its place of honor and long-standing grandeur, we feel strengthened by the ways it supports and celebrates our everyday lives.

Nourishing caregiver collaborations are just like this: gorgeous, important tapestries of collective care and consideration. Simple but awe-inspiring. Perfect in their imperfections. Individual but universal. And integral to the work we all do every day with children.

# Introduction: Families Know

## *"All Language Is a Longing for Home"* ~Rumi

When I was ten, my dad's eldest sister, my Ameh Joon Shokooh, lived with us for several months. She was visiting us from Sweden, where she had emigrated with her ex-husband from Iran before the 1979 revolution. She wore her hair ironed straight, which set perfectly against her turtleneck. She drank coffee beside me on a brown velour couch after school every day in our rented townhome in Monroeville, Pennsylvania. In my round, red-rimmed glasses and big sweaters, and sporting

*Nawal with Ameh Joon Shokooh, 1993.*

bangs, I would read aloud to Ameh from chapter books like the Nancy Drew series, sliding my finger under each word, exaggerating pronunciation for clarity. I would turn the book over to her and support her careful articulation of each syllable too, imploring her to stretch out the sounds. I was just in the fourth grade, and she was my first student. This was 1993.

That memory swims in my head among others from my upbringing as the daughter of immigrants in the United States. I routinely translated for my family at doctor appointments, filled out forms for them in waiting rooms, and broke down insurance claims to explain why we were charged a copay. I was responsible for all applications—anything from classes to renewals at the DMV, and for everyone in my extended family, too. As a young person, I questioned these added responsibilities, often lamenting the extra burden on my childhood. As I grew older, I felt guilty for bemoaning what I now know grew my identity, capabilities, and confidence. This sort of experience is written and talked about often among first-generation immigrants, and yet, it often goes unrecognized in the school setting as a literacy strength, let alone a springboard for more authentic classroom learning.

My mother's English was far from perfect, but she read stacks of library books to me aloud, sometimes inserting Farsi words. When I grew older, she told me that I often corrected her pronunciation, seemingly embarrassed by her "broken English" around my peers in Pittsburgh, which hurts my heart now that I know

how proud I should've been. But my mother was always a passionate proponent of the public library. Her father was a teacher back in Shiraz, and he had always dreamed of his children flourishing in the United States. When I could read to myself, my mother would drive me to faraway library branches where I could borrow volumes to complete the Babysitter's Club or Great Brain series. She encouraged me to sign up for reading challenges and even pushed me to get my first volunteer job at the library when I was sixteen. She spoke to me in Farsi, and I answered in English. Did these experiences toggling between languages and context not contribute to my acquisition of language, help me closely read complex text (and the world), and grow my critical questioning skills?

*Nawal's grandfather teaching in Iran.*

If my teachers had recognized these connections to literacy growth at the time, they might have seen my family as strong potential partners in learning. In fact, they could have centered those experiences to make my learning more relevant, immediate, and authentic. But because these connections were never made, these two aspects of my learning spun on parallel paths, never intersecting, and it wasn't until later in life that I saw how these experiences contributed to the shaping of my highly literate and language-rich world.

When I was forty, my dad's second oldest sister, my Ameh Shamsi, came to visit us in Jersey City, where my family and I had moved after living in Chicago for over a decade. It was a big transition—one we finally made to be closer to our relatives. We were sitting around the table, its leaves open to accommodate my parents, who were visiting too. My aunt took her time with breakfast: tea with feta cheese, dates, jam. At the same time, she took phone call after phone call from relatives in the Middle East, her cell phone constantly abuzz. This is 2023.

"I'm visiting Nawal in New Jersey," she'd say in Farsi, a little too loud. "The weather is good. I am not too cold. And you wouldn't believe how her house is so, so small!"

Over and over, she would repeat that my house is small, sometimes even passing the phone to me so I could *confirm* that my house is small. What solidified for me in listening to her is what I have always known: success in my family is oftentimes narrowly defined by material things—house and cars. Degrees and accolades. A successful marriage and children. What's missing in that definition are all the other ways to be, leaving space for alternative timelines, lifestyle differences, and new thinking. I don't blame them; I love my aunts. It's what they know because of how *they* were raised. It's how I was raised. Part of my journey as an educator is unlearning this.

These two vignettes of me and my Amehs are critical to understanding what I propose as an effort of collective care with the families of our students. How they define success is nuanced and varied. Those definitions of success determine how families spend their time, money, and efforts and have implications for how they navigate schools for their children. To embrace all caregivers alongside their children, we must realize that energy and efforts in raising children are often tied to parental hopes and dreams. And we must admit that misconceptions and myths exist about the literacy strengths of students whose families look different and about families' abilities to contribute. We all carry our own (sometimes erroneous) assumptions about our students' caregivers. Some of these are surface and superficial—snap judgments based on our own ideas of what's normal.

There was the time, when I taught sixth grade in the McKinley Park neighborhood of Chicago, that I assumed the mother one of my students stayed at home because she dressed so casually, when in fact she ran a massive bouillon cube operation. Because I never saw some of my students' fathers at parent conferences when I was an eighth-grade teacher in Brooklyn, I made assumptions about whether they were in the picture at all. And there was the time I mistakenly thought one of my students' caregivers was her mother, even though she was her grandmother. All of these assumptions sprang forth because I was raised in a specific context, with my own caregivers in *their* own context. We have learned to see the world in a way that is heavily influenced by how we grew up in it. All of these presuppositions that I made say very little about my students, but they say everything about me and the values that I bring to a classroom. When we consider values as they relate to classroom life, we realize a hard-to-digest truth: in many schools, English-speaking parents who learned how to do school well themselves tend to be "valued" more. They are seen as awesome partners and praised, whereas others are not. We are conditioned to believe the caregivers who excelled in formal education are the ones who will support their children the most. This harmful narrative simply isn't true.

Even more egregious is the purposeful erasure (inadvertent or not) of home languages and cultural rituals important to forming identity and the omission of whole, truthful stories of historically marginalized, underrepresented people of color. Many educators don't envision the Farsi-speaking mother of three who spends her days cooking, cleaning, and managing her household as a direct literacy partner, though I would argue her contribution is as valuable as a reading conference in the classroom. It is her rich recipe for noon-khamei (Persian cream puffs) passed down from other women in her family, orally explained, step-by-step, that builds her child's understanding of language and, more important still, identity and culture. This is authentic skill-building that shapes children and how they move in the world—and you can find an infinite number of examples of similar shared literacy experiences at home. When encountering caregivers whose educational experience or world orientation differs from our own, we must hearken back to the foundation of our own training and the very definition of what literacy is. Literacy is language—the ability to convey ideas with purpose and nuance and reach common understanding with others. Literacy is connecting with people through art, body language, facial expression, and sound. Literacy, at its most basic, is effective communication.

At its heart, literacy teaching is the teaching of what it means to be human.

When we step back to recognize this end goal and remember this foundational definition of literacy, we see all the ways that our students' caregivers can not only contribute but already serve as teachers themselves. Families in all countries, contexts, and communities have been supporting their children's language acquisition for centuries. They've been passing on traditions, expertise, and ways of knowing. This is a version of love.

> We are conditioned to believe the caregivers who excelled in formal education are the ones who will support their children the most. This harmful narrative simply isn't true.

Whether it is the executive managing a multinational business operation while traversing the globe, or the mechanic keeping a neighborhood of decades-old cars running so his neighbors can get to work; the hair stylist working until midnight the evening before prom so their young clients can have the night of their dreams, or the technician keeping a luxury high-rise cool during a sweltering summer heatwave— all of these adults have lessons to share with their children about the navigation of an ever-evolving, multidimensional world of language. They could

**At its heart, literacy teaching is the teaching of what it means to be human.**

not do what they do if they did not have literacy skills and language strengths worth recognizing. Many school systems consider "family involvement" through a deficit model lens, focusing on how families might not operate how we want or expect them to. This is a top-down approach, which can be exclusionary. As classroom teachers, we aren't getting the whole home picture unless we authentically commit to ongoing listening, learning, and relationship-building. It is the critical, compassionate work of dismantling our own biases that will break down inaccurate and harmful narratives.

Researchers have studied the myriad ways that families contribute to their children's learning at home, even if they're not always recognized. Homeschooler Akilah S. Richards recognizes the deep and meaningful teaching that happens, too, when adults give children freedom. In the unschooling journey of her daughters, she writes, "All they needed was space to decide on themselves for themselves, to go deep into different self-chosen and suggested areas of study, only and always with their consent. They needed boundaries not schedules, trust not textbooks. They needed to practice leading themselves" (2020).

Although I'm not suggesting unschooling our children, I do pose the question: How can teachers elevate what caregivers naturally do and transfer some of that freedom inherent in the way knowledge is built in those home spaces to everyday classroom literacy practice? One of our many roles as educators and school leaders is to exalt what families and caregivers do naturally to increase engagement, confidence, and literacy learning. After all, the goals of a caregiver and their children's teachers are so often the same. We want learners to be successful in multiple spaces. We want students to flourish in our home and school environments. We want our children to feel safe, loved, and willing to make mistakes as they move along their learning journeys. We want them to ask questions, collaborate with others, and be empathetic. We want for children to take care of one another—to understand that collective care sustains a more loving future. Our literacy ideals in the classroom do not exist in a vacuum. What we aim to teach and the experiences we offer must be connected to the everyday home and community lives of our students, with all their intricacies and nuances. And what we teach in the classroom *must* be applicable beyond classroom walls.

Student success increases when parents and caregivers feel invited to support their learners, which means they too have to know what our literacy ideals look like—both within the classroom and beyond, when students leave our care. Students spend 80 percent of their time outside of school (Afterschool Alliance, n.d.). The support they receive in these various settings grows their literate lives, as much as—or more than—what happens in the classroom. Insisting that every classroom assignment, activity, or task connects directly to the child's humanity outside classroom walls is one of the ways we can grow authentic communicators and provides a clearer bridge for caregivers to better understand the important role they play at home.

> Our literacy ideals in the classroom do not exist in a vacuum. What we aim to teach and the experiences we offer must be connected to the everyday home and community lives of our students, with all their intricacies and nuances. And what we teach in the classroom *must* be applicable beyond classroom walls.

Because families already meaningfully contribute to their children's literacy by being naturally and authentically themselves—in whatever language, with all of their beautiful rituals, customs, and cultural uniquenesses—this book aims to honor and amplify this deep work by sharing actions families can take to enrich what they're already doing. And it does so while considering the important truth—that we cannot assume families have access to resources, whether they be financial, social, and cultural capital or time. With that, I ask myself, what's the recommendation I can give to caregivers for whom time is their most limited resource, as it was for my own father, who came home at 2:30 in the morning from his closing shift at Domino's Pizza? What suggestion requires little beyond the rhythm of their day? It's not solely *my* suggestions to caregivers that will support their children in the classroom; it's their own intrinsic tendencies, often passed down from elders—the people who raised and supported *them*. It's their own brilliant competence with speaking, listening, and communicating that I aim to elevate.

After centering our conversations in respectful, loving practices in Chapter 1, each chapter that follows will focus on one critical tenet of literacy learning: process, community, observational literacy, talk, and choice. Together, we'll explore how the tenet shows up reciprocally in our schools and in children's homes across the following five considerations, grounded in a specific pedagogical stance:

◈ **Pedagogical Stance:** We'll open each discussion with a reminder that grounds the work in a mindset meant to focus our agency as teachers. Our task isn't about teaching a set of curricular documents or completing a checklist for parent engagement. You'll have to choose what makes sense based on your children, their families, and the context you find yourself in day to day. Nuance is simultaneously one of humankind's greatest gifts and griefs, as poet Kate Baer once said. When we open our minds to all the ways that our teaching—and our students, along with their families— is nuanced, we can teach more thoroughly and lovingly.

◈ **Listening:** As we journey together through the following chapters, notice how each is rooted in story and family parables, alongside lessons to learn and apply to our own teaching and caregiving of the students in our school communities, and vice versa. There is incredible power in our children's homes. Teachers learn from caregivers; caregivers learn from teachers. We all learn from each other.

◈ **Honoring:** This section will dive deeper into examples of ways the tenet is already present in our children's lives and homes. Notice how listening, learning, and asking questions to fully understand our students and their caregivers with deep respect is the first step to cultivating a strong and lasting family partnership that cohesively supports our learners.

◈ **Connecting:** Next is thinking thoroughly about already-existing home literacy strengths with an aim to grow students from that place, wholly. Naming the connection between home and school literacy practices is powerful. In this section, we'll clarify the tenet further while drawing a clearer line between shared family literacy experiences and classroom literacy ideals. We'll look closer at how a variety of instruction practices support it and, at times, consider how the reasoning behind these instructional moves and routines may not always be clear to caregivers. A list of recommended texts is also included here for educators to share with students and families to grow their thinking about each holistic literacy tenet.

◈ **Exalting:** There is a strong *instructional promise* that exists when we dismantle the traditional top-down model of family engagement. Instead of schools telling caregivers "this is how you can help us," discussions in this section will exalt existing family practices and will show how we might enhance student growth from a place of enthusiasm, through purposeful, simple suggestions for families to continue to grow their children as they are.

◈ **Inviting:** Our goal here isn't just about inclusivity or one-off "family engagement" or "literacy night" events. It is not an afterthought to be bolted on after unit design and lesson planning. Instead, we can weave family literacy engagement into every aspect of our educational approach and ask the critical question at each juncture: What role can our caregivers play in reinforcing this particular skill or strategy? What are families already doing to grow this in their authentic settings? In this section, we'll explore strategies for inviting families—with easy-to-implement suggestions and examples—into our shared literacy goals. Whether it's through text suggestions, questioning scaffolds, modeling in education spaces like labsites, or entries into our curricula, these invitations will help you show families how they can weave further and more intentionally into their students' school literacy lives. This part concludes with several suggestions you can communicate via newsletter, during conferences, in catch-all updates, or however you see fit. All families are different, so you'll know best how these recommendations will land and what adjustments might be necessary. The suggestions are not exhaustive, nor do they apply to all caregivers; they're meant to get you started.

◈ **Reflecting:** Each chapter will conclude with reflection questions that support your excavation process to build deep and meaningful connections between home and school. These reflections will help you think about ways we can learn from and incorporate natural family literacy practices into stronger, more engaging ways of teaching our students. And more than that, the reflections are meant to remind us of what's most important: growing the whole child's confidence and capabilities in communication while centering their full, beautiful humanity. Because this is an important part of your personal growth, feel free to spin off from the included graphic organizers into webs, lists, or any meaningful think space you find most useful for you.

The work of including *all* families is a foundational endeavor to teach *all* children. We cannot profess to value learning for every human if we do not value the site of every human's initial and most enduring learning—family. The beings that define home and the experiences that they provide are all so profoundly different.

We know this. Yet, when many of us consider these terms, we default to thinking of our own homes and our own families. These thoughts become the reference points that help us define "normal." For humans, the things that feel closest to what they had or have feels "normal." Comparatively, everything else becomes different, abnormal, and divergent.

These thoughts on differences become our first biases. And we all have them. On impulse, "biased" can feel like a dirty label or an attack. This is not the case here. To suggest that we all have biases simply means that we all have established patterns of thinking that lead us to certain conclusions and actions. If unexamined, those biases can result in conclusions and actions that can harm people. If explored thoughtfully, understanding our biases becomes a gateway to the kind of critical thinking and inclusive behavior that can change whole school communities.

> We cannot profess to value learning for every human if we do not value the site of every human's initial and most enduring learning—family.

My father worked outside the home—several jobs at a time, which contributed to my understanding of "normal." When I encounter fathers who do not work, it takes my brain just a few extra seconds of reflection to remember that this is "normal" too. My mother spent every night scratching my back and telling me stories. When I encounter mothers who work evenings, away from their children, it takes my brain just a few extra seconds of reflection to remember that this is "normal" too. Families are different.

This is an important concept to remember throughout this book: that "normal" is not universal. Each of us has an idea of "normal" that comes from the culture in which we grew up. Our routine preference for the things that feel most familiar to us is a bias. We can learn to see beyond them. If we are to have schools where every family belongs, we must.

There is hope in embracing reflection.

"Neither our evolutionary path nor our present culture dooms us to be held hostage by bias. Change requires a kind of open-minded attention that is well within our reach," writes Jennifer L. Eberhardt, a social psychologist and researcher of implicit bias. "Our brains, our minds, are molded and remolded by our experiences and our environments. We have the power to change our ways of thinking, to scrub away the residue of ancient demons" (2019). Eberhardt contends that one way to correct our brain's bias automaticity is to slow down and force analysis, to move from the primitive to the reflective.

To include all families, with their wildly differing experiences, psychologies, and perspectives, as true partners in our literacy classrooms, we must unpack internalized biases about what families look, act, and sound like. Because I went to a mostly white private school among students with high economic status, my family needed an invitation to feel included and valued. To attend an event was a big deal for my parents. They tiptoed around my teachers and other families so as not to draw attention to themselves, always wanting to look perfectly manicured. My dad was embarrassed to show up in his food prep uniform. Standing out or critically questioning things was taboo to them. We were "lucky" to be there. Other families didn't move with this kind of deference, behaving instead as if the school belonged to them. They acted with the expectation that teachers and other families would make the kinds of decisions that benefited them. When they didn't, their complaints were direct and consistent.

This is probably a tension in your school too. Some parents have voices we desperately want to hear, whereas others' we hear too much. Some families' wishes for their children are silenced behind walls of shame or fear or nervousness. Others' wishes for their children are apparent on every PTA agenda and in every school policy. This tension dissolves the bonds that hold school communities together because it ensures that the people who already feel at home there receive all the benefits of that community. The people who feel like outsiders in that community continue to exist at the margins of it. Part of our work as caregiver-minded educators is recognizing that this tension exists and that working through it is oftentimes quite public.

This tension is further complicated by gender, class, race, and ability. In a country where white values and culture are often accepted as "normal," those who are most fluent in these values are often the ones who have the most access to the benefits associated with school. Those with different values, practices, and circumstances often get less.

Teachers, we can disrupt this.

We must refuse a singular approach for engaging with and communicating with families. What remains constant across all interactions with families must be an acknowledgment that all caregivers want the best for their children. Families are already providing thoughtful literacy and language support, in their own ways, infused with love—telling stories, growing knowledge about the world, and teaching their children how to read situations and experiences in ways that directly support literacy growth in the classroom.

> What remains constant across all interactions with families must be an acknowledgment that all caregivers want the best for their children.

Without the belief that all families and caregivers have these strengths—even when home and community experiences look very different from what we imagine or are used to, even if their definitions of success do not match ours—we cannot form true partnerships. And, most important, we cannot authentically reach and teach the whole child.

# Chapter 1
# Celebrating Families' Intrinsic Knowing

When I visited Iran as a child, I would stay at my grandparents' home in Shiraz, where my mother grew up. I barely remember the first of these visits—I was only a toddler—but the photos we have of that summer create memories that haven't left me.

By the wide stone steps in the back courtyard, plants grew rampant, and the wash would get done, either clothes or vegetables or rice. I recall holding the hose, my mother guiding me. I'm not sure what I was washing, but I remember the voices of my elders—and their eyes on me. I kept filling the plastic basin, then carried it to the threshold of the door. My Baba Ghambar watched me with wonder but eventually intervened, placing a small kilim at the edge of the stone stairs. I'm not sure if this was so I wouldn't fall and hurt myself or if it was to sop up the extra water. It was a very small act of knowing. And it made a huge impact.

Kilim rug patterns can be asymmetrical, which some people view as imperfect. I know, though, that there is value in every kind of rug, just like there is value in every kind of knowing. My grandfather's act of support—laying down a kilim between the courtyard and the home's back entrance—

*Nawal in her grandparents' backyard. Shiraz, Iran. 1983.*

taught me what it meant to be safe. Maybe he was trying to teach me how to prevent water from pouring over into the house; maybe he wanted to protect my bare feet from the too-hot, sun-heated stone. His knowledge was simple; his teaching indirect. In this chapter we ground our thinking in the pedagogical mindset of searching for and leveraging every kind of knowing, weaving it into the contours of our teaching thread by thread.

## Families Know

When I was in second grade, in 1989, I used to walk home with my dad a few short blocks from Mt. Lebanon Elementary School. I remember a chalk pink backpack slung over one shoulder with a lined piece of paper in my hand, perforated edges ripped wrong, head down as my father berated me for spelling *babies* wrong on a ten-word spelling test. "Why would you write *babbies*?" He asked, shaking his head, seeming truly baffled. "That says *bab-ees* . . . and your handwriting is sloppy. Doesn't the teacher make you rewrite this?"

Fast-forward three and a half decades and I'm walking again, now as an adult and a mother of four. My friend Rachel and I are bundled against the cold on the 606 recreation trail in Chicago, large, hot teas in hands, in the midst of a pandemic. She hands me a belated birthday gift: an auburn knit hat with a cream-colored poof on top. "You know," she tells me, "I can't get Adrian to read anything other than junk. It's all *Captain Underpants* and graphic novels."

These vignettes aren't a critique of my father or Rachel's parenting, but they reflect a persistent disconnect between what caregivers believe strong classroom practices *look like* and what we know as educators *is a more holistic practice*.

And in many decades, little has changed.

The conversations we have with caregivers today still reflect the same biases, assumptions, and concerns that I noticed in my own parents thirty-five years ago, even though our teaching methods are more powerful. Perhaps we educators haven't done a good job communicating with caregivers what we know is at the heart of literacy instruction: a love of words, authentic reasons to write, idea-building above polished finals, process writing over prompts, student talk above teacher lectures—all in addition to building an independent reading life founded on interest and intimacy. Classroom teachers today might ask students to decide on their own actions after reading, to create a visual story in response to learning, to decide what genre they want to write, to collaborate in book clubs. Teachers might ask kids to lead. If you are teaching in a workshop model, mini-lessons are likely taught as whole-group, keeping direct instruction short, so learners can think and work afterward to grow their literacy muscles. And then the real work begins, with kids doing the heavy lifting by practicing genre strategies independently and in small groups while teachers confer, meeting each child in a differentiated manner to support individual growth. In a reading workshop, students might read their choice of independent book in lieu of a whole-class novel, and teachers might meet with them individually to ask questions, apply skills and strategies to that independent reading book, and practice thinking side by side. This literacy classroom structure looks different than it did three decades ago, and even as you read this, instructional practices are continuing to evolve. But do caregivers know that? This is no different from the information you take to a new doctor who collects a history of your health and ailments. To support you and keep you healthy, it'll take the intentional merging of your doctor's expertise and your personal knowledge of your body and what you've experienced. Sometimes a school's expert knowledge and the wealth of information caregivers bring simply do not match. It is part of our work to ensure they do.

Perhaps the choice and autonomy in a more holistic vision of literacy instruction, which are foundational in so many of our classrooms, are what caregivers are ultimately confused by. We need to demystify for parents and caregivers our latest literacy practices so they can better support their children. Remembering that kids spend more of their time across the year at home with caregivers than they do with us in schools, a true caregiver-teacher partnership is one of the most important pieces of the instructional puzzle facing schools today.

Caregivers, like all of us, are deeply human. They are multilayered beings who are not all bad or all good; they are learning, making mistakes, growing, and changing over time. We have to remind ourselves to resist labels or assumptions about who they are or how they parent based on a small number of interactions, a single event, or a minor sample of data. Nobody should be wholly labeled for isolated occurrences. I speak from personal experience, as a mother who sometimes snaps at my children, cries when I feel overwhelmed, smiles often, and wonders constantly if I am making the right parenting choices. My own father is incredibly supportive but often lost his temper when I was young. Should he have been reduced to his singular parenting missteps? Never. He was unconditionally loving and faced an enormous array of challenges as an immigrant navigating life in a new country. He reflected, grew, and parented my younger siblings differently. It's important to look at patterns and change over time.

> Caregivers, like all of us, are deeply human. They are multilayered beings who are not all bad or all good; they are learning, making mistakes, growing, and changing over time. We have to remind ourselves to resist labels or assumptions about who they are or how they parent based on a small number of interactions, a single event, or a minor sample of data.

## The Ways Families Engage with School

Similarly, we must recognize that every school and community are different when it comes to experiences around family engagement. There are different communication methods, reasons for connecting, events across the school year, assemblies and volunteer efforts, and timing for parent/caregiver conferences. Underlying all that, we have relationships that may or may not feel respectful and positive. In 2021, when I interviewed Chicago school leaders during a parent literacy engagement pilot program for the city's Department of Literacy, at least half of those interviewed reminded me that their students' caregivers faced educational trauma themselves. And trauma like this, or even just a general sense of uncertainty, can manifest in a variety of mindsets that families consciously or unconsciously bring with them as they engage with school systems, including those shown here.

| | |
|---|---|
| **Fearful Engagement** | Caregivers who engage fearfully with school tend to operate from memories of when the institution of school itself has been harmful. Actions made in this stance are organized around minimizing suffering, embarrassment, or loss. "No contact with that place unless it's absolutely necessary . . ." Every interaction in this stance is filtered through a sieve of potential distrust and the expectation of possible harm in the future. When caregivers come to us with this mindset, it's important to remember that building trust will likely take time, affirmation, and consistent, nourishing efforts. Families have to see tangible and frequent evidence of the benefits of engaging with school. Moreover, they have to see their own children thriving in ways that they themselves did not in school. |
| **Tentative Engagement** | When considering the frequency and quality of time spent engaging with school, tentative engagement can look like fearful engagement on the surface. Both result in limited caregiver connection to school. Tentative engagement, however, comes from a different place. Families engage tentatively because they have more important, immediate, and pressing things in their lives—very human needs—other than school stuff. For example, they might have a graduate degree that they're working on at night, or trouble putting food on the table, or infant twins they need to care for, or an elder in the family who needs them, or a second job that they had to take to pay the rent. Our families are all carrying so much. School is a vital priority to educators, but it cannot always be the central priority to families. Life happens, and many of our caregivers are carefully rationing the energy that they have to invest in things beyond the home. When our practices send messages of shame and judgment (even if unintentionally) for investing in the necessary things that are not school, we weaken the already fragile connection to school spaces. In many instances, this can result in compliant engagement, which can rise from feelings of guilt for not doing enough and leave families and caregivers feeling unvalued. We can combat this by creating multiple means of access to school for families. Historically, the focus here has been: "let's make this convenient for parents." In this book, we'll push toward making meaningful and accessible connections with families. How can engaging with school connect to graduate work or provide outlets for our elders or sharpen the job search? |
| **Compliant Engagement** | Compliant engagement is performative. It is not valued beyond a data point for the school or meaningful at any true level. Schools tout their parent attendance numbers often, but few real connections are ever made in this stance. Caregivers involve themselves out of a sense of duty, not from a place of curiosity, love, or community-building. Many school stakeholders think that this shallow participation is what engagement looks like. Caregivers who are compliant do what they're supposed to do because that's what school says they're supposed to do: show up to the events, talk to the other parents, contribute to the fundraiser, send supplies when asked, and volunteer at the carnival. Compliant engagement is often shallow and leaves caregivers feeling empty, because it's not connected to a real sense of belonging or the actual life of their student. |

*(continued)*

**THE WAYS FAMILIES ENGAGE WITH SCHOOL** *(continued)*

| | |
|---|---|
| **Transactional Engagement** | Transactional engagement can show up in many different ways, but it all stems from the same value: entitlement. Families with this mindset might believe that they mean well, but they often come across as thinking that school exists to serve their family alone, even if that comes at the expense of other families because their family deserves it. Transactional engagement is reductive, generally including only those who are "in the know" or in the "right" social circles. Families who have a transactional relationship with school often overwhelm school systems with calls, emails, and suggestions to the teacher or principal, pilfering the already limited time we have to serve students. Yes, we need involved, supportive parents. But sometimes that "involvement" costs us time, energy, and communal goodwill. We can combat this by emphasizing community and collaboration as opposed to competition and opportunity hoarding. |
| **Toxic Engagement** | Toxic engagement happens when any of the aforementioned forms of engagement go unaddressed for too long, despite our best intentions. It leads to disengaged silences or articulated hostility between and among members of the community. The good news is that this, too, can be addressed with careful planning and open communication. |

The ways that families engage with schools vary widely based on a variety of factors. It's important that we eliminate judgment. Indeed, one of the most powerful comments I heard in a Los Angeles workshop I facilitated for school leaders named the realization that family engagement does not need to happen *at school*. Sometimes the most important work we do to bring families into the fold aims to further engage caregivers with their students *at home* and in their communities. It's important, then, that we deconstruct the false parallel that education equals schooling, and instead embrace the everyday ways intergenerational learning happens in family and informal settings (San Pedro 2021). This book is a journey away from fearful, tentative, compliant, transactional, and toxic engagement toward the kind of collaboration that is nourishing, affirming, and healthier for all families.

> **Sometimes the most important work we do to bring families into the fold aims to further engage caregivers with their students *at home* and in their communities.**

School is a social institution. As such, it shares all of the shortcomings of the society in which it is situated. A society that does not fully value the contributions of women breeds schools that have difficulty ensuring that all girls thrive. A society that makes war on its poor condones schools that criminalize them.

A nation that cannot recognize the humanity of BIPOC folks is home to schools that dehumanize them. Parents of children from historically marginalized groups know this, and they engage with school wielding that knowing as either a weapon, a shield, or a disengagement tactic. And they are not wrong in this. This is historically responsive behavior. We can build school experiences for all parents that write new histories of how we serve together in school communities. Building on the research of Janet Goodall and Caroline Montgomery's parental involvement continuum (2013) as well as Karen Mapp and Paul J. Kuttner's dual capacity-building framework for family-school partnerships (2013), my work with teachers adds story and nuance to the ways we collaborate and invite families into our work, making it evident from our very first communication that:

◈ all caregivers add value, no matter what their life experiences are or have been

◈ teaching authentically and holistically means shunning a transactional, fear-based level of engagement

◈ meaningful connections are the only way to meaningfully learn

I also know that it gets complicated. Caregivers might not feel comfortable coming to the school building for any number of reasons, and these can be compounded when you consider the historical ways gender, race, and class have affected parental engagement. These truths are critical to keep in mind. Maybe your school tends to invite families in when students get into trouble. Maybe your school has established and longstanding processes for bringing families into the fold in meaningful ways beyond one-off PTA events. Either way, the key to building strong, positive, and respectful relationships with caregivers is to ensure they feel their innate power—authentic, rich, and generational—with clear intentionality and invitational conversations.

Think about the most marginalized, least-heard parent voice in your classroom community. Would that person feel comfortable asking questions? Would they know what to ask? How would they feel showing up for parent nights, report card pick-ups, or other events? For caregivers to feel safe and valued, with a sense of belonging, we must invite each one into our collective work in nourishing ways grounded in the shared goal to grow their children as literacy learners.

## The Things We Know: Every Family Does Literacy Already

This book seeks to exalt all families and support all teachers. For that to happen, we weave together the knowing of both. I want to arm you with techniques for recognizing and communicating strong literacy ideas with every kind of caregiver, all of whom love their children, inherently want to do right by them, want to know how they can help, and, more often than not, have questions about what will ensure their children's growth and positive development overall. In essence, this book is a toolkit for communicating with families and tapping into the unbelievable literacy strengths that reside in *every* child's home.

And make no mistake: there are literacy strengths in EVERY child's home.

I come to this work as a former public classroom teacher in two major cities—Chicago and Brooklyn—as an adjunct professor, and as a longtime literacy coach. As a classroom teacher, I fielded questions from anxious caregivers worrying about their eighth graders who struggled with reading or their younger kids who didn't readily write. As a literacy coach, I am consistently asked to facilitate workshops for caregivers. I support teachers with holistic literacy instruction in public schools, charter schools, and Catholic schools, in suburban districts, and from the highly affluent to the most underserved. Before teaching, I spent time with families in all walks of life as a newspaper reporter.

If journalism opened my eyes to the inequities of the world, education shone a light on them. It became increasingly clear to me who is privileged and protected, and who is not. I wanted to be a reporter because of the social responsibility—because it felt like a critical role to play for social good. But I felt ineffective. I could not make real change as a reporter. It felt like all I did was say over and over again that things were unfair. Wrong. Harmful for children. But I was just *saying* it. I wasn't *doing* anything. Now I know that teaching can be just like that: a whole lot of *saying* and not *doing*, unless we consciously fight to interrupt traditions that constrain us.

As a mother to four multiethnic kids ranging in age from four to twelve, I struggle every day with the pressure of deciding what is best or right for them when it comes to learning and education. And, like most families, their father and I want to raise compassionate, critical thinkers whose curiosities are piqued, who will contribute to their communities and care about the world around them—and the people in it. As a parent, I have discovered this: kids learn when we deeply listen. Kids learn when given choice, voice, and agency. Kids learn when we pay careful attention to what they're telling us—in every way, not just verbally. Our kids learn with strong modeling, plentiful examples, and really clear demonstrations. Powerful teaching is built on this knowing, as is powerful caregiver and home engagement.

Our kids learn despite us, too, showing up with different home experiences that lay the foundation for *who* they are and *how* they learn. I often joke that my fourth child, Eloisa, is the most verbose and has the strongest problem-solving skills and that it's because we've largely left her to her own devices. As a baby-turned-toddler at the height of the COVID-19 pandemic, she breastfed during my Zoom calls, absorbing the conversations I had in every meeting alongside me. Her first words were, "Mama, charger," as she teetered toward me with my laptop cord. And as the last child, Eloisa has had a very different experience from Eliana, our firstborn, whom we doted on with lessons from all kinds of baby classes. Eloisa is more verbal than them all, and it didn't take pricey efforts.

Crafting literacy-rich moments with our children—for all families—should feel deeply rooted and sustainable. Every example in this book comes from the communities where I serve, know, and love people. The parables I share throughout are the things that feel effortless in the moment. They are part of caregiving, part of our collective ancestry, and part of our community legacies. The time we have is sacred. Our task, together, is to celebrate what already exists so that families understand their power, while also considering ways we might invite them to support their children's literacy growth even more. We must bring additional awareness and intentionality to what families already do—and have always done.

## Families' Intrinsic Knowing

Most families have traditions, routines, and habits that—when we think about them—elevate language practices. In my house, we share "roses" and "thorns" around the dining table to tell stories about the day. A friend of mine moves conversation around their dinner table similarly but calls the anecdotes "ups" and "downs." More recently, at my daughter's conference, her teacher, Javier, added a third

### THERE'S MORE THAN ONE WAY TO BE LITERATE

If we see literacy as only singular, we limit the range of kids' expression, and by doing that, we limit the range of their learning. In the twenty-first century, we understand that reading is more than just text on a page and writing is more than just symbols on paper. In the twenty-first century, someone's ability to read a text can take them only so far. They have to use those very same skills to read relationships, interactions, and institutions. The same facility that we hope kids bring to character analysis, we want them to bring to understanding their communities. The same proficiency kids use to navigate plot and motivation is the same understanding we want them to bring to their comprehension of why people in their world do the things they do. Because the world is so multifaceted, our understanding of literacy needs to be, too. In a world where kids and families often feel excluded, our literacy practices can ensure that everyone is included. For further reading, check out David Kirkland's scholarship: *Rewriting School* (2021).

branch: "buds," which highlights places with room to grow. My kids recently added "weirds": delightful acknowledgments of the inevitable, strange moments that often unfold across a day.

At night, when I scratch Eloisa's back to help her fall asleep, I tell her stories about me and my cousin Sahar when we were very young, washing doll bums in sinks and making hideouts in the bushes in the side yard. I tell her about Uncle Jalal's rice-eating sleepwalking behaviors and about Uncle Nezam getting smacked across the face at a Khorramshahr bakery, which propelled my irate grandfather to shut down the town's single spot to buy bread for the week. Though these stories are true memories, I start with the Farsi *yeki bood, yeki nabood*, a Persian version of *once upon a time*.

**The time we have is sacred. Our task, together, is to celebrate what already exists so that families understand their power, while also considering ways we might invite them to support their children's literacy growth even more. We must bring additional awareness and intentionality to what families already do—and have always done.**

Our families know. I think about the medical study that proved mothers can tell their babies have fevers more accurately by hand than most thermometers (Teng et al. 2008); how caregivers know at school pickup how the child's day went with one look at their body language; I think about how intimately we know our own children. And I think about how all of these things are part of the natural way caregivers communicate, in ritual, practice, conversation, and reflection, that are critical ingredients in literacy learning. Chicago-based author Samira Ahmed builds stories with her children when they walk to school, one starting with a single line and the other adding to it, until a full story unfolds. My childhood friend Sarah, a psychiatrist in Pittsburgh, concocts word problems about cereal box nutrition, connecting stories to math at the breakfast table. My friend Francesco amuses his children with Italian humor and games. He animatedly enunciates every word, so slowly sometimes that his English-speaking wife, Katie can understand what he's saying. And families all over the world sing nursery rhymes in different languages. They do these things naturally.

There are children learning language at their grandmother's knees, getting their hair braided, listening to wisdom from the past. My friend Acasia grew up listening to her mother sing gospel at funerals, which she says shaped her own love of words, drawn out, staccato, soulful. Watching my friend Chris-Annemarie quip with her sister and mother, I recognized the innate strength in that Jamaican patois inserted every couple of phrases: familial, identity-shaping, intimate.

I observed her young children absorb their grandmother's language lessons while they ate mango at her feet. I know how my own children join me in belting ballads, depending on my mood, sometimes broody and deep: Toni Braxton's "Unbreak My Heart" and Lauryn Hill's "To Zion" among our regulars. These rituals grow their literacy lives.

Children everywhere add to their full linguistic repertoires simply by being in their community, like my own son, who has been raised on the barber shop banter where he went weekly in Humboldt Park, Chicago, with his father for a shape-up—now too in Montclair, New Jersey, since we moved back East.

All of these varied language practices come naturally and, at the same time, truly elevate what we try as literacy educators to achieve: discourse, fluidity, curiosity, problem-solving, and an ability to gather knowledge and move accordingly afterward. Family ways of being and knowing are rich and multi-layered. These family "funds of knowledge," a term coined by Luis Moll and colleagues when they studied Mexican American households in Tucson, Arizona, recognize that caregivers contribute greatly to their children's learning experiences. Beyond simply counting the number of books in their households, their research celebrates the deep knowledge in children that stemmed from at-home interactions that included carpentry, first-aid procedures, consumer and culinary knowledge, and longtime family rituals, which inevitably contributed to the child's growth and well-being (1992).

As I reflect on all of these stories, it leads me to one conclusion: in love and chaos and everyday weirdness, families know. They know because they live lovingly. They know because they navigate chaos. They know because they make mistakes. They know because they persist by consistently learning from them.

 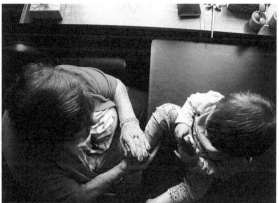

*Intergenerational wisdom.*

## The Things We Do: Relationships First

Schools that strive for nourishing caregiver connections know relationships come first. They build them. They convey interest and ask questions, and they communicate openness. Cultivating relationships with students and their families means understanding and honoring their journeys, identities, and rich histories. This often means inviting families into the classroom in person or virtually, and not just at the start of the year. It means going to great lengths to understand caregivers who don't speak English, to make sure those adults understand us, and to translate classroom communications as needed. It means drawing from the deep brilliance that every caregiver scenario offers children. And it means making additional, easily incorporated suggestions to ensure families feel more confidence in what they're already doing to strengthen their children's learning journeys, regardless of the time they have available or their financial means. But all of these efforts—indeed, all the suggestions included in this book—fall flat if they aren't grounded in respectful relationships.

Every individual wants to be seen and heard; every child matters. That is another truth we know. Centering student stories at the start of the year includes engaging in research around who they really are and finding ways to share their stories in the classroom. Successful relationships also begin with a genuine curiosity and interest in the other person's journey. It begins with listening and asking questions that show a desire to know, learn from, and grow each individual child.

If possible, visiting home spaces virtually or in person often gives us wonderful insight into the richness of each child's upbringing, who is caring for them, and what their current family situation is. Then, we'll want to ask questions that lead us to deeper understanding, still:

◈ What is their cultural heritage?

◈ Who does the child have relationships with, and how did those relationships shape them?

◈ What language practices are in their homes?

◈ What experiences are the children navigating?

◈ What literacies are they adept at negotiating beyond alphabetic?

◈ What spaces are caregivers building for their children that springboard rich and authentic learning experiences?

◈ Are children bilingual or multilingual, and do they translanguage by inserting other languages into English expression?

◈ Are they visual, lyrical, amazing at tactile and sensorial building?

◈ What does each child do especially well?

◈ Do they travel to visit family and friends?

◈ Are their people in a country currently experiencing political upheaval or revolution, war or trauma?

◈ Do extended family play a role in their lives, and do they live close or far?

We ask these questions because we know each one shapes our students and, in turn, our understanding of their caregivers and empathy for what they currently experience. My father is Arab and Iranian, born and raised in the southern-most city of Iran at the Iraq border, with Bahraini roots; my mother is Iranian. One side of my family speaks Arabic and Farsi; the other speaks Farsi alone. I'm not sure whether the fact that I am multiethnic was ever discovered or explored by my teachers when I was in school—not from the perspective of knowing my parents, and not from the perspective of understanding my identity as a student. Are there ways we can invite families into our classrooms to share of themselves, their backgrounds, their rituals and their cultures?

## The Things We Do: Open Communication

To build strong partnerships, we need to be thoughtful about our communication. *What* we communicate and *how* we communicate it can send hidden messages about what we assume and what we value. By swapping out the traditional Mom and Dad with "your caregivers" or "your grownups," we are being intentionally inclusive. Instead of saying husband and wife, I now say partner or spouse. To embrace more inclusive ideas around gender and for households with two mothers or two fathers, we can avoid automatically defaulting to he/she and instead say they/them for pronouns. Instead of parent/teacher conferences, I encourage districts to adopt caregiver conferences or family conferences, which is more accurate and welcoming for all family arrangements. We send an even more inclusive message of deep care when we ask families and children what they want to be called and what they call each other. Let them share their preferred terminology. For example, I call my cousin Sahar my sister, since we were raised together and are only two months apart in age. Though they might seem simple and small, these important considerations and language shifts send messages of loving respect and bleed into everything we do.

I'm the kind of person who has my phone in my back pocket at all times, not only for work but also because I have ongoing chains with friends and family, ones laden with important information, ones that make me laugh. We communicate with GIFs and emojis and all kinds of capital-letter shouting and often in different languages. But I have mama friends who toss their phones in a drawer when they come home and refuse to peep at them till dawn. Because they're inundated with work emails, some of my friends never check emails on their personal accounts during the week. If you want to reach them, a phone call on their way home from work might be your best bet, or a face-to-face conversation at daily school drop-off. As educators, we are definitely maxed out on time. But wouldn't it send a message of goodwill and respect to get to know caregiver communication behaviors and choices so we can better and more easily reach the families we serve? When I was a classroom teacher in Brooklyn, I would go to the spot where I knew some of my students' parents worked, like the bagel store on the corner, just so I could share time. We've gotta do what we've gotta do.

*What* we communicate and *how* we communicate it can send hidden messages about what we assume and what we value.

In my experiences with families and caregivers, both as a newspaper journalist who interviewed in homes and as an educator, I learned that face-to-face communication increases space for respect. Although recognizing that some families might have boundaries around in-person communication, it begs asking caregivers upon meeting at the start of the school year if they would be amenable to it. Though it's not always possible, I strive for in-person interactions that can eliminate tone confusions, which often arise when we rely on email for sticky or even innocuous conversations. Body language is communicative. Empathy increases. Miscommunication decreases. A mass newsletter or email to the class list doesn't always feel like the direct connection parents sometimes seek in person or via phone call. The sentiments we wish to communicate through methods like these—that children are personally cared for and known in school spaces—sometimes don't come across as well as they might in person, no matter how well-meaning and effusive we are with our words. When communication breakdowns do occur and there are disputes, heightened feelings, inconsistencies, and confusion around grades, behavior, or something else, it is even more essential that educators are communicating with families personally and directly.

When I was a sixth-grade classroom teacher in Chicago, I'd block out time Thursday afternoons, before I carpooled home with my colleagues, to call families and praise something their children did. It was an effort to garner goodwill and build positive relationships with my students, not necessarily their families. I wanted them to know that Ms. Q would reach out to the folks who love them if they were out of line and needed more support, but more important, Ms. Q would tell it like it is for the good stuff, too. What I remember most about those afternoon phone calls were the distrust and dismay parents would express when answering the phone, worried that the only reason a teacher would call was because their kid was in trouble. What I learned was that I built trust by praising students.

In all of this, we want to continually reflect on the hidden messages our communications might imply. As you consider the various modes of communication we typically use, presented in the next table, think about the potential messaging we might be sending. This might look different based on your school and the resources available to you. I've described it in ways that have worked for me and my schools, but please remix and reimagine these ideas in ways that work best for your communities.

# Caring Communication

| Mode | Content | The Message It Might Send |
|---|---|---|
| Email/ newsletter Paper/newsletter going home, for the fridge | Here's what we're doing in class. Here's how you can extend the learning at home. Questions to ask your child before, during, and after reading | The teacher wants to tell me what my child is learning at school. The teacher is making suggestions for what I can do to help my child at school. The teacher is too busy for face-to-face check-ins. |
| Text: to individuals or mass, via What's App or Remind App | Logistics, reminders Praise | The teacher doesn't want me to forget a bagged lunch, a themed event, a shortened school day, and so on. These reminders help my child's activities run smoothly. The teacher is using multiple modes of communication in a real effort to connect with families. |
| Kid-created parent update either via voice note or video, sent via text or email | Something they accomplished that they were proud of in the week Example of work that they liked to do | My child is proud of their growth and accomplishments, and the teacher has built a space to ensure they can share that. The teacher is teaching the children to explain their own classwork, learning, and maybe even process. |

*(continued)*

CARING COMMUNICATION *(continued)*

| Mode | Content | The Message It Might Send |
|---|---|---|
| Face-to-face meeting/sharing time | Praiseworthy moments and individual concerns that need to be addressed | The teacher appreciates my child's uniqueness and growth. The teacher values in-person, authentic interaction and makes time to address my concerns. The teacher really wants me to hear this. |

## Communicating Interest: Asking Loving Questions

Now that we've talked about how to connect with families, we can think about earnestly getting to know them. We want parents to know we care about their children and believe in the power of our partnership. How do we get to know incoming families, year after year? What sorts of things do we want to know to help us better care for and grow their children? You could send a Google form, ask families to send in a video or audio recording/voice note (always easier for me, given constant time crunches, and so easily digested), or schedule quick virtual meetings. In-person run-ins at school pickup or drop-off windows work, too.

When we relocated from Chicago to Jersey City to live closer to family, it was incredibly eye-opening to experience the new student intake for our four young kids in their varied new school settings. We had everything from emailed questions about our family and our child's interests to absolutely no communication or knowledge of who we were or why we had relocated, what our children had just experienced in the summer transition (multiple apartments and crashing with family, etc.), or otherwise. One morning, I remember my daughter cried during the entire leaf-strewn walk to school because she was worried about her off-color uniform tights, and when her teacher saw her and asked about it, she was surprised to learn we were still living out of our summer duffels while our belongings sat in a Chicago storage unit.

The following questions that we might ask when new families join our communities serve to understand the child, their background, their uniqueness, and their journey. They aim to center loving positivity and student strengths with an eye toward growth:

◈ What languages are spoken at home? What languages are interspersed or peppered in?

◈ When and where at home does your family engage in language building, storytelling, conversation, and reading?

◈ What stories do you enjoy telling?

◈ What do you enjoy doing alongside your child?

◈ What passions do you have that you share with your child?

◈ What knowledge (about your family, community, ancestry, or culture) do you want to ensure your child learns?

◈ What sorts of "texts" do you "read" as a family (e.g., video, sound, images)? (This question taps into a broad definition of what it means to read.)

◈ In what ways does writing show up authentically in your household? Do you write letters, thank-you cards, recipes, lists, instructions, signs, or labels?

◈ Is there anything in particular you're worried about or want me to pay careful attention to with your child?

◈ What cultural traditions, religions, holidays, history markers, and celebrations are important to you?

◈ What's the best way for me to reach out to you? When is the best time?

## Communicating Openness: Inviting Loving Questions

I have friends who are so unclear about what's happening in their child's classroom that they have to piece things together, based on kid commentary, and draw their own conclusions. And, when papers come home, they tell me they often have no idea what to ask. They know not to home in on grades alone, but they're confused about the learning that resulted in the artifacts that make their way home in backpacks. At that point, the trust between caregivers and teachers might already be tenuous.

This brings to mind an important point: communication between school and home isn't a one-way street. It should be cyclical and reciprocal. As we ask caregivers about literacy at home, so do all caregivers need to feel comfortable asking us questions about their children's literate lives at school—about their children individually, about classroom culture, and about the instructional decisions we make. There isn't a week that goes by without my getting asked by a friend or a friend of a friend about their child's literacy learning, their child's teacher's approach to teaching, or further clarification about a typical classroom practice, from *How do I make my child a stronger reader?* to *What is a workshop approach?* to

*Do graphic novels and audio books count as reading?* These are folks who know I spend time in dozens of schools; these are people who have the social capital to inquire. I also have friends who feel they don't have the right to ask teachers questions, or feel they can't approach teachers about instructional decisions because they don't know what's right. They don't want to be perceived as not knowing what's going on, when they're really just worried about their kid. Most of the time, the caregiver who reaches out to me will start with the caveat: *I don't know if this is legit but . . .* or *Help me understand—what's up with the teacher asking . . . .*

Think now for a moment about all the different children you serve. Do all families have a friend like me that they can ask these kinds of open-ended questions to? Do all families feel they have the words and the power to ask questions of their classroom teachers that will further elucidate their understanding of literacy growth? Do all families have the time to engage teachers without feeling ashamed for not knowing, or not having the time, or not knowing the "right" way to support their kids? One way to build relationships with families is by explaining from the start that they can and should ask questions, whether for clarification, making suggestions about their children's literacy learning, or further understanding our classroom ideals. In interviews for my work with Chicago's Department of Literacy, I discovered that school leaders want families to understand *both* how the academics work in the classroom *and* the generally joyful and lifelong literacy practices like reading for pleasure and writing for authentic reasons. Likely, you feel the same way. Families and caregivers should be privy to information about grading and curriculum, but not only that; *all* caregivers should understand the role literacy plays in their children's lives and how they might advocate for that. And, to this end, they should feel invited to ask the questions necessary to get the answers they need to do so.

To help, teachers in many of the schools where I coach arm families and caregivers at the start of the year with a set of suggested questions to ask, each stemming from a holistic approach to literacy learning. As you look across the chart that follows, which questions prompt a need for further reflection on your part? How do they align with the holistic literacy moves you want to ensure are part of your classroom? What would you add to this list that might further elevate family strength and connection to learning?

# Questions Caregivers Might Have About Their Child's Literacy Experience

| Individualized | Choice/Voice/Agency | Process/Growth |
|---|---|---|
| What does my child do really well? | What topics is my child interested in learning about? | How has my child changed as a writer over time? |
| How does my child learn best? | What interests has my child shown in the classroom? | How has my child grown as a reader? |
| What inspires wonder and awe in my child? | Where can you show me examples of my child having choice in expression to share artifacts of learning or choice in mode of composition? | Where can I see examples of my child engaging in the writing process? Where can I see examples of their writing across the genres: narrative, nonfiction, opinion? |
| Who does my child work best with? | How do the ways you know my child outside of school show up in the classroom? | What kind of reflection does my child engage in? |
| How does my child speak up for themselves in groups? | How does my child know the purpose of each lesson or activity, and why it's important beyond the classroom alone? | What opportunities does my child have to share their work with a wider audience outside the classroom? |
| How does my child participate and share about themself in class? | What opportunities are available for my child to use their full repertoire of language skills in reading and writing? Where is translanguaging (or insert another language fluidly) encouraged? | Where is there space for collaboration with peers in my child's literacy work? |
| What services is my child entitled to at the school, and how can I learn more about those services? | Does my child know that you know these details about them? | How are you helping my child to initiate their own reflection? |

## Communicating Access: Classrooms as Welcoming Spaces

As a journalist I was trained to be the eyes and ears of readers so they too could learn what I learned on the beat as a reporter. Our role as educators is similar, to share with caregivers what is happening in the classroom so they can see what their children are learning. Most of our parents and caregivers would love to be a fly on the wall in our spaces. Context matters. When caregivers better understand what's happening in the classroom, they feel empowered to better make connections for their students at home. If we provide context for the artifacts of learning that get sent home, caregivers are inclined to ask their children and school systems more informed questions. We can fill families in on our classroom literacy practices and content with a weekly email, newsletter, or bulletin, but sometimes short videos or voice recordings with a summary are often easier for families to quickly digest. In the schools where I work, these follow a predictable structure to honor everyone's lack of excess time. Even I am guilty of too-quickly skimming a teacher newsletter and clicking the delete button, but a voice recording or two-minute video often seems easier.

No matter the mode, we typically include the following components:

◈ **Summary** of weekly learning, told in the form of reading, writing, speaking, and listening strategies that are applicable beyond classroom walls. *This week we learned strategies to . . . One of the ways we learn from nonfiction is by . . . These strategies will help your children when they . . .*

◈ **Extension** ideas for the home, either with suggested questions or some form of the strategy practices mentioned. *You might support your learner by . . . You might ask your child . . .*

◈ **Opportunities** to get involved, either in regularly scheduled programming like being a mystery reader for the day or a bigger ask such as curricular connections based on family member expertise or interest. If we tap into our caregivers' passions, hobbies, and abilities, we can not only provide unique experiences for our students but also boost caregiver confidence and build stronger rapport in education spaces. I've had parents who know how to make soap, dance salsa, speak Tagalog, and knit scarves come into classroom spaces during various reading and writing units. Questions we ask families at the beginning of the year help us learn what my students' caregivers know and love to do that we can then consider as we plan across the school year. Be mindful that folks might not deem their everyday behaviors or hobbies valuable for classroom sharing, so it helps to provide a list of examples that you build on every year.

◈ **Direct requests** for questions, ideas, or suggestions for upcoming class-room concerns, or clear decision-making points that affect the community. For instance, setting up "listening hours" for families and caregivers to drop by and have a conversation with you about recent challenges their children are facing is a wonderful way to not only build relationships but clarify caregivers' questions.

Exalting families and their intrinsic strengths is part of our responsibility as educators who care for children. It is part of how we connect with the identities of our students; it is part of how we understand better how to grow them. This is about unconditional, positive regard for all caregivers.

The truth is this: families know. They have always known.

We just need to listen.

# Reflecting: Celebrating Families' Intrinsic Knowing

| List some typical questions you generally ask families and caregivers: | What potentially hidden messages (positive or negative) do each of these questions imply? |
|---|---|
| | |
| **List some typical questions families and caregivers generally ask of you:** | **What larger concerns or unasked questions might these indicate or invite?** |
| | |
| **List some typical home-school connection efforts you and your campus tend to have in place:** | **Reflect on each entry, asking yourself what values, assumptions, and messages each might suggest.** |
| | |

## Reflection Space

Feel free to use this additional space to process the reflection
questions and your own thinking from this chapter.

# Chapter 2
# Process: The Journey
# *Is* the Learning

In summers when I was a kid I went to a day camp at a
school near my house. My days there were all adventure and
learning, curiosity and fun. The counselors were intentional.
Each week they celebrated a specific theme. There was an
ocean week, a volcano week, and a nutrition week. I'd return
from camp full of new information, insights, and experiences.
The day my counselor announced that they would be having a
Middle East week was probably one of the best days of my life,
because as the *only* Middle Eastern kid at camp, I felt seen.
We were promised Middle Eastern art and dance and food
and language.

When I look back years later on how Middle Eastern week
was planned, I'm a bit scandalized by the lack of nuance. It
glommed so many groups and people under a single umbrella.
My counselor started with Middle Eastern tapestries. My
thoughts raced back to the warmth of Iran, and handwoven
tapestries my family have there; how exciting that my camp-
mates would now know the same warmth. They would know
the careful selection of fibers. They would know the naturally-
dyed colors and the ritual calm of weaving in and out row
after row.

What my counselor presented was not this. Her supply bag was filled with red plastic looms right out of a Walmart clearance aisle. This was not my culture, and I wanted nothing to do with this cheap approximation. I was too young to protest with my words, so I let my inaction communicate my disgust. All day at camp I sulked and did nothing. I looked forward to going home and communicating my rage to my father.

It surprised me that he did not share my anger. Instead, he responded with a lesson about the process of learning. "You don't even know the details of Bedouin weaving," he told me. "Expression is, at best, an approximation. Your counselor was giving her best guess, but because you were mad that her guess did not match yours, you missed a real opportunity to learn. What the tapestry looks like from culture to culture changes, but the weaving itself? That part is unchanging." Because I was more concerned with the final product, I had refused to engage in the learning process.

No two kilims or artful tapestries are alike, just like no learners are alike. No two school years are alike. Though you might teach the same units, they'll look different because each year the classroom community is different. This is part of your process as a teacher. In this chapter we ground our thinking in the pedagogical mindset that the process of learning is more important than the final product.

## Listening

Last holiday season, my son was given a large Lego castle. He spent days in his room building it, paging carefully through the extensive directions, tearing open each new step's bag of pieces without so much as looking up to see who was around. I beamed with pride as I passed his room hour after hour where he sat rearranging the pieces, his brow furrowed deep in concentration. He made changes to the castle that weren't in the instructions, explaining to me as I passed why he opted for a diverging pattern. We had to bug him to come downstairs for food, and he ignored his sisters. When it was complete, it was an intricate, multilayered masterpiece. After days of work without cease, he carried it down the stairs to show off to us all. But, as if in slow motion, he tripped, fell down the bottom two steps, and smashed the massive building into the teeniest of Lego bits and pieces. The thing was utterly shattered.

I felt like crying—I almost did. But he didn't even care. He may have flinched, but no tears followed. Instead, he shrugged his shoulders and said, "It was really cool," started picking up the pieces, and asked for a snack. My daughter and I looked at each other in disbelief. I jumped up, an "It's okay honey, I'll help you fix it," on the tip of my tongue. How could he have spent days on this design and not care one bit about ruining the final product?

*Ehsan's castle.*

The truth is, Ehsan had enjoyed the process. He valued the thought and work that went into putting it together. It was not about the final result. He's not the kind of kid who has shelves of completed Lego designs on display—he builds for hours, then dismantles and tries another iteration.

When I tucked him into bed that night, I couldn't help but ask how he felt about accidentally demolishing his hard-earned creation.

"You okay, azizam?" I asked.

"Yep, why?" he asked, unfazed.

"Your castle . . ." I began.

"Mom, it was fun to build" was all he said. "And cool to think about making it better."

That's when I realized it was my internalized desire for results and my discomfort driving the conversation, not my son's displeasure over what happened. I wished I could be more like him. That night in bed, I stared at the ceiling. I couldn't let go of this truth my kid was teaching me.

As a mother, I felt pride in my child's behavior that day. But my feelings as an educator were hard to reconcile, as I thought on repeat: why did it hurt me so badly that his final piece was gone, seemingly created in vain? Why did it bother me that he spent so much time on something for which he had nothing to "show" but a throwaway line about the process being fun?

In the darkness, I thought about how often Ehsan makes sketches of superheroes and villains: my little left-handed ten-year-old, scribbling in all sorts of notebooks, only to crumple them and try again with new colors, markers, or movement lines. He'll see something in a book that he would like to try, so he'll add to previously tossed-aside drawings, taping bits and pieces together like a true artist. I realized this kid almost never cared about polished final results to display or show off.

## Honoring

What was it about Ehsan's castle-building process *without* a final result that felt so unsettling to me? My mothering side flushed with pride; my educator self struggled. Here's where I landed: kids have a natural inclination to be in process, but because adults in school value and reward the final product, children learn, over time, to care about the things that make the adults around them happy. Product. Perfection.

When I leaned into my caregiving mindset, I knew instinctively that it would serve my son well later in life to value the process he takes to get somewhere, instead of solely admiring the final result. When I was young, I remember sitting mouth agape when my Maman Ghanieh taught me that you need yogurt to make yogurt. I would watch with awe as she spooned a tablespoon of plain yogurt—sour, homemade—into heated milk, leaving it to sit in mini bowls in the turned-off oven. We would go together to check on the little yogurt bowls throughout day to see if it was just right, the way my family liked it: tart, firm, perfect. We'd bring the little bowls to the dinner sofreh in the evening to eat alongside dill rice and tahdig. Of course, the final product was delicious and resulted in something my family felt we could get only in the Middle East, but the process of creating something new alongside my grandmother was everything. I loved watching her dip her pinky finger into the substance to test readiness. My dear friend Elana talks of learning to knit alongside her grandmother, sitting on a reupholstered couch on the west side of Milwaukee. "'Loop the yarn around and pull it off one hook onto the other,' she'd say, with her hand over mine. I don't remember what we made, but to this day, I remember the process. There was comfort in it. It felt like a gift of knowledge she was handing down to me."

The truth is, home lives are rife with examples of natural processes that our children are witness to and intimately involved in. Our kids might observe the growth of a plant at home, either potted inside or outside in their communities. They might notice the process of a baby sibling or cousin changing over time; of a building facade slowly deteriorating; of their own growth at a sport or activity.

I do the same with my recipe making, reworking parts of Persian stew steps that are too time-consuming. Though my father expresses dismay at my inability to follow my mother's measure-by-hand instructions more precisely, he has admitted more than once that my reimagined versions turn out just as delicious. This is how creativity and ingenuity work: taking suggestions and thoughtfully envisioning new iterations that are more our own. We want to cultivate these literacy-rich skills in our young people. It's important for our children to know how to follow directions, but it certainly is not *the* most important thing. If I'm being honest and wearing my mama hat, I want my children to *know* about the instructions but be able to make their *own, informed* decisions about how and when they follow them, based on context, consequences, and their own determination of what's best. With these real-life stories of process, revision, and growth in mind, we can better design classroom literacy learning, in ways that connect the home and school.

How can this happen, though? How do we shift our classroom practice to value process in a school ecosystem that mainly values finished products like grades, projects, and test scores? It starts by thinking, as colleagues, about what we value and what we want our students to experience on their way to meeting the standards.

## Connecting

As we move toward being more in-process with children and families, we can reexamine the things that have kept us tethered to perfection-as-mindset for generations. It is hard to deny that we live in a results-oriented society. Whether executives evaluated on share price gains or day laborers paid for completed work, by the time we reach adulthood—and even before then—we are taught that it is the outcome that matters. The outcome is what determines our compensation, our progression; for some of us it is hard-wired into our sense of self-worth. Parents tell me all the time, "I work in the 'real world.' There's no room for imperfection in my job. I just need my kid to get good grades." This is a harmful way to be—especially for children—because it leaves no space for the imperfection associated with growth.

The truth is that school is not the world. There needs to be space for mistake-making, innovation, and iteration, even if those spaces do not exist in other institutions. We do not prepare children for a broken world by inviting broken practices into our classrooms. This simply creates harm. We prepare children for the world by giving them the tools to imagine and forge more human, loving realities.

Depending on your own historical and cultural perspective, you might think the goal of process is perfection, you might avoid mistakes, you might unintentionally take over the collaborative work when planning with groups—all of these can affect both how families feel invited into our collaborations and the importance of process in learning that they interpret from the messages we send. For this reason, it is critical that we analyze our own stance on process versus product (and how this affects our actions in the classroom) so that we can consistently help our caregivers reorient how they view their children's educational progress.

> We do not prepare children for a broken world by inviting broken practices into our classrooms. This simply creates harm. We prepare children for the world by giving them the tools to imagine and forge more human, loving realities.

Teachers might inadvertently underscore this mentality of perfection. For example, sending home only completed, graded work—emphasizing the results of assessments over the continuum of gains made over the course of a school year, or a child's reflection on how they've grown across time—reinforces this outcome-driven mentality that many adults already bring to their children's education. There are alternatives.

We know that funding for education is dictated by standardized test scores that are not commensurate with actual learning. Test scores make or break budgets, and administrators have to prove learning in standardized ways within a system that is neither equitable nor flexible. Those tests do not measure what's most important, nor is it solely the final result that matters.

Skillful literacy educators who embrace authentic home and life literacy experiences know what matters. Oftentimes, they don't feel equipped to fight the mandates. Educators might know in their hearts that slowing down, observation, reflection, and deeper analysis of how learning morphs across time are literacy tenets to exalt, but they feel pressure to meet ever-moving learning targets and cover a too-wide breadth of curriculum. If you feel like that's you, you aren't alone.

Plenty of literacy practitioners believe (and design their practice to support the belief) that the journey and reflection of the learning process are equally important, if not more important, than results, particularly when it comes to tests created *without* all children in mind. This is true for both reading and writing, as we strive to show students how to lift the level of their reading comprehension, conversations with peers, and written compositions. Before we can begin to have this conversation with families and suggest ways they might support their children's growth over time at home, it's imperative that our actions and what we signal to children in the classroom underscore this ideal.

We can start living these values in our classrooms by weaving process points into every part of the curriculum:

◆ naming the learning explicitly,

◆ saying why it matters,

◆ and intentionally planning for student reflection.

For example, for a recent essay assignment, instead of just having kids turn in solely the finished product, I asked them to videotape themselves explaining their thesis to a partner at three different points during the development of their writing. Later, I asked them to compare the videos to see how their reflections evolved. I wanted them to see how much more effective their conversions became over time, with practice, and how these changes looked across the year. I invited students to consider reflective questions to prompt their thinking about how they've grown using the following questions to prompt them to think about their evolving processes when it comes to communicating and sharing ideas with peers. To the process-oriented practitioner, student reflection is as important as the essay.

◆ What do you notice about the attentiveness between you and your partner? Look at all the ways you're paying attention. Are you leaning, looking, talking with your hands? Are you nodding?

◆ How would you describe the level of ease in talking to your partner? How did it change?

◆ What examples did you and your partner give each other in the videos?

◆ Which video seems more comfortable, and why?

◆ How did you grow as partners from the beginning to the end of the quarter?

## Kid Conversations: Out Loud or on Paper

To make additional connections beyond these in-class videos, we might ask students to talk about their most successful conversations outside of school or in other school spaces, like the lunchroom or play yard. I've heard children talk in these scenarios about challenging peer conversations they had to navigate and

*Partners talk about growth over time. Fifth-grade students in Chicago's Pilsen neighborhood.*

then reflect on how they eventually made it work so well. We often think of these discussions as falling more in the realm of social work or the counselor's office, but when we're committed to collective care, this *is* part of holistic literacy work. Crafting space in the literacy classroom for reflection about our students' social worlds helps us break down walls between what constitutes school processes and real-life processes, which is critical for their growth.

My own 12-year-old on a recent morning was explaining how hard it was to be sure two of her friend groups didn't feel slighted as she fluidly decided who to walk home from school with. "Mom, I felt really bad. I didn't want Annie to be left out, but I know she doesn't get along with Miriam. I didn't know what to do."

I listened. I reminded myself not to rush to solve.

"And then what happened?" I eventually asked, when the silence felt long enough.

"Nothing. I think it ended up being okay," Eliana told me. "Maybe I'll take turns walking them home. Maybe they'll eventually be friends. I kept sorta thinking it was a right-now problem."

When we celebrate conversations as a process that changes over time—like a muscle we can grow with practice—we are connecting authentic literacy practices inside and outside of school. Authentic reflection on student growth over time can be fostered as part of the classroom's systems and structures, beyond the traditional checklist or compliance-oriented version of self-reflection.

In our aim to create classroom cultures of collegiality, community, and camaraderie, we can ensure that, first, the feedback we give students in literacy lessons and their independent application conveys our support of each student's process and the varied ways each child grows over time. Collecting student work in an online or physical folder like a portfolio is a step, certainly, but carving out time for students to consider their progress is critical. For instance, our mini-lessons should include language around reflection, looking back, reviewing past work, and explaining how change happens. If we're teaching a writing workshop, for example, we might look at how a small idea morphs into a draft and grows stronger with each revision. It's not the final product alone that we should display, share out, and amplify. Rather, we might display one part of each iteration and have students orally reflect on how their writing changed across time.

I love how Maureen Murray, a middle grades teacher in Chicago, has her students annotate their final writing pieces with sticky notes to name what writing moves they tried. In this way, we honor the process and celebrate change, while communicating with our actions that final results alone aren't the heart of literacy learning.

When we regard all kid conversations as valuable, we are communicating a holistic and process-forward value to teaching. We're saying: you, wherever you are on your journey, matter most. And your growing is part of your learning.

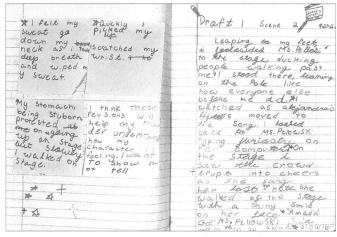

*Annotated student work.*

## HOW PERFECTIONISM HARMS CHILDREN

Authentic learning requires approximations and room to make mistakes. Learning is iterative: we learn something and then try it.

The first attempts at anything are never perfect. Never.

The first several tries are always messy. Always.

With any endeavor: Cooking, sports, school.

The thing that leads to good or great is repetition and reflection on what did not go well. Simply put, if you remove imperfection, you remove learning. More transparently stated, if you remove imperfection, you remove humanity. This is a form of oppression because it robs children of the chance to get good over time. This opportunity theft is especially pernicious when it is directed toward groups that have already been historically denied opportunity in institutions like school: girls and women, BIPOC, queer people, people with disabilities, and those facing financial distress.

The mindset of our current competitive culture has erased the necessity of imperfection from schools, giving the illusion that learning is a direct progression from teaching to perfect execution. This is most powerfully exemplified in some toxic workplace cultures. Adults are sometimes denied opportunities to learn or time to get good at a thing. Profits, mandates, and deadlines come before actual learning. Both people and institutions suffer significant learning losses in this scheme.

*(continued)*

**HOW PERFECTIONISM HARMS CHILDREN** *(continued)*

Even though we may know (and feel) this, in too many school contexts, we impose this belief of "instant perfection" on children. Even when we don't say it with our mouths, we say it in our grading practices or classroom policies. We try to excuse this harm by telling ourselves that we are "preparing them for the 'real world.'"

One of the most important things we can share with caregivers is that we don't prepare children for the real world by replicating this toxic culture. Instead we teach into students' strengths and skills and support them as they encounter the productive struggle necessary to truly own their new learning. This process requires space for imperfection. For more information, read Tema Okun's scholarship at WhiteSupremacyCulture.info.

## Adults and Mentors as Imperfect

You can elevate the idea of process culture in the classroom in other ways, underscoring for kids growth-mindset and mistake-loving environments (Cruz 2020). I position myself in front of children and my preservice students as wildly imperfect, vulnerable, and always learning. If I don't know the answer to a question, I name that directly; if I am trying out a new lesson or idea with kids, I am honest about that method being a brand-new trial. The most powerful tool I've learned as a teacher is to say out loud: *I'm not sure. Do you want to figure it out alongside me?*

This learning stance is one that kidlit creator Jasmine Warga says anchors her books for young people. "I don't see my books as giving answers," Jasmine told me, especially when the topics are weighty. "Instead, I feel my books are saying, 'will you think about this with me?'"

In the classroom, I solicit student feedback and make changes according to their opinions on what worked and what didn't, so they can see more directly an evolution of process in the way I teach. They can observe my learning before them as a critical part of my humanity. In my college-level syllabus, I make changes when necessary as I get to know my students better. I want these preservice teachers to see the importance of being flexible with their processes, that learning their students helps them know better what and how to teach. In fact, I often conclude our semester together by inviting them to describe what felt most useful, and why. I try to model what I want them to see and be. For the young people in our care, this is most important: we are all gorgeously human. We are all in process.

# More Ways to Explore the Power of Process

Sharing learning experiences together while exploring a variety of resources will always be one of the best ways families can support the power of process. Here are a few favorites to keep the conversation going with kids, caretakers, and educators.

| Text Title | Author |
|---|---|
| *The Camping Trip* (2020) | Jennifer K. Mann |
| *How to Write a Poem* (2023) | Kwame Alexander and Deanna Nikaido Illustrated by Melissa Sweet |
| *She Persisted* series, both picture and chapter books (various) | Various authors |
| *Calling the Moon: 16 Period Stories by BIPOC Writers* (2023) | Edited by Aida Salazar and Yamile Saied Mendez |
| *Emergent Strategy: Shaping Change, Changing Worlds* (2017) | Adrienne Marie Brown |

## Process in Literacy

The reality is oftentimes our actions as teachers don't align or communicate to children and their families the value of process in literacy. We might *say* it's important to notice how we grow as readers, but then we communicate grades based on reading level or tests alone. We might *say* that growth matters, but we celebrate children who came in knowing or overpraise students with the means to showcase their final projects in extravagant ways. How often do we inadvertently send confusing and misaligned messages like this to students?

For instance, I recently overheard one fourth-grade student wondering why his teacher red-penned his draft of a speech for student body president, when the audience would never see his writing anyway. I'm sure his teacher valued process in his writing, but that was not communicated by her actions. Wouldn't it have served the learner better if his teacher supported the growth of his ideas and oral organization instead? What did an emphasis on handwriting and spelling alone, in that instance, communicate? Why did it even matter what was actually written, if the speech delivery is what ultimately mattered for this persuasive piece?

Caregivers might look around today's literacy classrooms and wonder why they don't look like the classrooms they learned in, which often included store-bought decorations or traditional displays. In our conversations with them, we'll want caregivers to see the value of a coconstructed classroom that exalts process, which means potentially bare walls at the start of a school year. When we coconstruct the classroom environment alongside students instead of printing store-bought or online materials alone, we inherently share the importance of authentic learning processes. In classrooms I've supported, as students learn reading and writing strategies, they make larger visuals as reminders of their literacy tools and decide where in the classroom those materials live. Teachers periodically make time for students to review the classroom environment (with scavenger hunts to find answers in charts, for example) and have students together assess what visuals are useful for either creating the learning space they need or cultivating a stronger sense of community, as is the case with photocopying the covers of favorite read-aloud books and decorating walls with them as a physical imprint of the class journey.

Students create labels for their classroom libraries to organize book bins. They coconstruct the classroom contract of norms and behaviors that lead to safe and respectful learning environments. To see a classroom at the start of the year already decorated solely with store-bought or printed Teachers Pay Teachers charts that often get overlooked by students likely signals to caregivers an environment more centered on aesthetics than being coconstructed as a place of belonging with the students in our care.

## Process in Writing

Finished writing that we often send home with children is the result of a long back process of brainstorming, drafting, revising, editing, polishing, and sharing, but this journey can be invisible to families if we don't highlight and celebrate it for them. It may not be clear that writing processes aren't always linear, or that a whole variety of skills may have been taught along the way. If you're teaching a writing workshop, you will likely have many lessons for idea-collecting and an equally large number of strategies for revising. When we're thinking about making connections with families, and we send home only a final piece, caregivers remain outsiders to that learning process. We're missing the visual representation of how the child got to a final product or how they made countless, critical decisions along the way. This is especially true in the cases of students with different learning abilities. It is important that caregivers learn the scaffolding we've provided for their child to lift the level of their writing and thinking.

Families may be surprised to learn that editing and polishing usually include fewer lessons than revision, because we're more focused on process and the final piece isn't the most important point. A child who grows their ideas from scratch, moving along their own growth line, should be celebrated for whatever changes they accomplished. It may not be clear that we celebrate attempts to replicate and remix mentor writing moves and praise thinking about how to communicate more clearly. Or that, when conferring with young writers, we might choose to forgo surface fixes such as spelling and punctuation so we can focus on process-driven questions that fuel excitement around the ideas.

An example of a writing process classroom chart, which can be shared with caregivers, too. Hand-drawn by Maureen Murray.

Conferring with teachers and peers supports students' abilities to narrate their revision process, explaining why they made writerly choices across time. I absolutely love having students narrate alongside their final drafts how they *came* to that result. They can name the writing moves they tried to improve the piece and how they made part of it audience ready (Coppola 2019). However we choose to emphasize the importance of change over time in writing, our communication with caregivers should highlight a focus on idea-building above all else and the importance of students reflecting on their writing process over time. More considerations to clarify around writing instruction are included in Figure 2.1.

**FIGURE 2.1**
*Process-Focused Writing Instruction to Clarify with Caregivers*

| Writing Instructional Practice | What Might Not Be Clear to Caregivers |
| --- | --- |
| Sending home process pieces across a writing unit instead of solely the final composition | It might not be evident to families that a lot of work went into the creation of a written piece, that the child brainstormed their own idea and likely drafted then revised more than once and likely revisited the writing multiple times before making the piece that caregivers see. This might create an erroneous assumption that some kids arrived to class knowing, as opposed to showing how much students grew over time. Sharing examples of all parts of the writing process—brainstorming, drafts, revisions, edits, and on-demand writing—is a strong way to communicate with families how students' repertoire of writing strategies evolves over time. |

*(continued)*

**FIGURE 2.1** *(continued)*

| Writing Instructional Practice | What Might Not Be Clear to Caregivers |
|---|---|
| Teaching many genres of writing across the school year | Caregivers might not realize or remember from their own educational experiences that writing instruction includes showing kids how to find story ideas, convincingly command an argument, or share knowledge about a specific topic. Based on how they learned writing in school, they might believe writing is more formulaic, with requirements on the number of sentences in a paragraph or length of an essay. |
| Supporting student revision of ideas during the brainstorming and drafting phases; leaving spelling, punctuation, and grammatical edits to the editing phase | When teachers focus heavily on grammar, spelling, and punctuation during the part of the writing process meant for idea-building, we inadvertently emphasize surface fixes that—let's face it—in the real world can often be addressed by computers. Conversely, when educators give feedback to students on revision strategies, organization, and communication of ideas (before we get to the editing and polishing stage), families and caregivers receive the message that cultivating strong communication skills is of utmost importance. |
| Supporting students in oral recording to narrate decisions they made as writers, whether replication of instructional strategies or writerly moves they noticed in mentor texts | Name clearly for caregivers why reflection on decision making is critical for student growth. Families often do not understand how important this is for growing young writers' abilities to make effective decisions about their compositions so they feel pride, ownership, and command of their own communication skills beyond the classroom. |
| Cultivating many strategies for deciding what to write about and giving students choice about their writing topic | Caregivers likely do not know that in some classrooms all students are writing about different topics that they self-select based on interest. Sharing with families the underlying belief that all students are authors who can find ideas for what to write about helps caregivers know that writing is not a teacher-constructed classroom activity. |
| Hosting celebrations and showcases for student writing | The idea of having a writing celebration with a wider audience beyond the classroom community might be new for families and caregivers. Perhaps they haven't seen writing units that focus on process, taking four to six weeks of diligent strategy-building, peer collaboration, and student reflection. Perhaps they are unaware of how many times writers revisit a piece of writing, or they don't realize mentor texts can inspire and support student writing—all of which bears celebration. |

## Process in Reading

In similar ways, process for reading means trusting that with instruction and joy, every child will learn to read, love to read, storytell, and listen to stories. It means trusting that a cumulative building of process will, across time, contribute positively to children's literacy and language development. When I think about communicating with families and caregivers about process, I want to speak to their potential anxieties or insecurities, pushing back against mainstream narratives about being "behind." We know that all kids grow and learn at different rates. Talking about a kid being at "grade level" is a necessary shorthand of the profession, but it ignores the reality of differences among children. This is an important conversation for teachers to have with families: to explain that children are where they are, without labels or judgment, and that our jobs are to grow them wholly. Variance exists between children and when they learn to read, even (especially) among siblings. My own four children had wildly different reactions to our book-reading rituals and their own evolutions with reading, and they had the same literacy coach mama the whole time. Reading slumps occur; there might be moments when you wonder why, after doing everything you can, your child still doesn't love to read. Reader advocate Donalyn Miller reminds me that "reading will always be there"; there are times when even adults don't have strong reading streaks. Here's when we must assure families and caregivers that the various experiences they naturally provide in the home combined with the skill-based instruction that we provide at school—reading strategies, letter sounds, vocabulary, critical thinking skills—all contribute to reading growth over time.

This is when we tell caregivers that yes, audiobooks count, and that kids can reread books for reassurance and comfort. Books on repeat fill us with fortitude. They're warm security blankets. They're solace. And for our youngest, who might not fully know how to read alphabetically yet, their memorization and memories of having the book read aloud by grownups in their lives support their early literacy foundations so they, too, can read the stories to each other, even if they're relying on picture-based retelling at this stage. My four-year-old, Eloisa, asks us to read Oge Mora's *Saturday* (2019) several times a week. And though I can grow tired of rereading these beautiful stories on repeat, I recognize what this rereading process means for Eloisa. We want all caregivers to understand that we celebrate experiences like reading to siblings, playing with words, and having books read to us again and again as part of the process of becoming lovers of literacy.

Another way we showcase process in reading is by helping children see how their reading lives have changed over time. We encourage students to think about chunks of their lives, depending on their ages, and ask questions about what they liked to read at each point, what stuck, what stayed. We remind them that the term *text*, again, can be expansive here. It can and should include comics, shows, music, and images of food, places, and more. We point out that every step on their text journeys counts toward our experiences with language, and it's important for caregivers to know how deeply personal the reading process is and how each one of us has varied home lives that shape and dictate what resonates on that journey.

> We point out that every step on their text journeys counts toward our experiences with language, and it's important for caregivers to know how deeply personal the reading process is and how each one of us has varied home lives that shape and dictate what resonates on that journey.

Figure 2.2 shares a handful of process-focused reading practices we might employ that may need to be clarified for caregivers. What other practices would you and your colleagues add to this list?

**FIGURE 2.2**
*Process-Focused Reading Instruction to Clarify with Caregivers*

| Reading Instructional Practice | What Might Not Be Clear to Caregivers |
|---|---|
| Conferring with students during independent reading about their reading plan and goals and what's working and what's not | Caregivers might assume that our conferences are casual moments where we "just talk about books" and may not understand the intentionality around these conversations. Take time to show them how these check-ins specifically help students focus on their reading goals and plans while giving you a chance to do some individual informal assessment. This can be done by emailing out a video of a reading conference in the classroom, modeling a conference during a back-to-school night, and sharing during progress report or grading time how the conferences led to differentiated instruction for each child. |
| Building stamina for and scheduling time for long uninterrupted blocks of independent reading | Caregivers might be under the assumption that some kids just "like to read" and others "just don't," when there are myriad other factors that contribute to a child's reading stamina, including their desire to read the text based on choice, their match with it in terms of ability, and whether they're able to focus within the learning environment. Parents may not know that building reading stamina is akin to building any muscle: it takes diligence and repeated practice. In interactions with caregivers, suggest setting a timer and celebrating increments of increase when children happily read for longer periods of time. |

FIGURE 2.2 *(continued)*

| Reading Instructional Practice | What Might Not Be Clear to Caregivers |
|---|---|
| Encouraging choice in book selections and genre studies | Invite caregivers to observe how much more interested and engaged their children are when they are able to choose what they watch, who they spend time with, and what their day looks like. When we give our children agency to make decisions for themselves, they are able to follow their intrinsic curiosities and read to learn about what they want to learn about. Would adults want to be assigned what to read, and would they do it willingly? Through offering choice, we message to students that their opinions matter, and learning is thus more authentic. |
| Asking open-ended questions that prompt larger debates as opposed to basic plot-based and summary-driven questions | Make sure to communicate with caregivers that plot-based questions and retelling prompts alone are lower-level learning outputs that suggest rote answers and require less critical thinking. Although it is important for students to know where to get information and answers from the text, and comprehension is key, supporting children in thinking beyond the text for context and why its message matters allows transference and application for lessons in other everyday life situations. Because we aim to educate students beyond classroom walls, building abilities for discussion and respectful debate among peers is of utmost importance. Support families in using critical thinking stems that elicit more than just "yes" or "no" answers, such as: Why do you think the author wrote that? How could the character have acted differently? How is what you learned different from what you initially thought? |
| Allowing students to select options for responding to texts in ways that matter to them | Perhaps because of how they were schooled themselves, caregivers might believe there is only one way to respond to text: by filling out answers on a worksheet or in a textbook, writing an essay, or answering multiple-choice questions. When students are given the opportunity to create their own responses to text based on what compels them—in the ways that they feel compelled to do so, whether visually, orally, on slides, or on paper—they are being given space to authentically digest and learn. When we as educators and adults dictate a specific way responses need to look, we hinder the child's ability to imagine. But, when encouraged to do so, students will usually think beyond our reach. |

*(continued)*

FIGURE 2.2 *(continued)*

| Reading Instructional Practice | What Might Not Be Clear to Caregivers |
|---|---|
| Leaving room for readers to abandon books | I felt freed when, as an adult, I learned that I could abandon books that did not suit my needs at the time. Like everything else in life, reading is deeply personal. Sometimes we may not be able to carry the weight of a text's heavy content. Sometimes we may not enjoy the writer's style. Sometimes, a book might be triggering, or remind us of something painful we'd rather bury at the moment. Students need to know that abandoning books, within reason, is acceptable. Communicate with caregivers the important truth that abandoning books does not make for a poor student and that, if it becomes a pattern that prompts concern, you'll address it in an individual conference with the reader. |

## Elevating

When I think about my own upbringing, my family avoided some conversations. My parents were seemingly direct and honest, but I know too that we just didn't talk about some topics.

Maybe this is because they didn't want to admit they didn't know clear answers, either. Maybe their parents never talked about tough or sensitive topics with them. Either way, it would've served me well to hear the ways my parents navigated difficulty. I would have loved to know their ups and downs; I would've loved to hear what they tried and where they failed.

At this point, you might be thinking about how your parents handled confrontation when you were a child. How they talked through uncomfortable conversations. How they explained family challenges, and how you got through them.

Not all caregivers find it easy to talk to their children about challenges they themselves faced in life, let alone hardships they're currently facing.

But sharing openly with our children (as appropriate) the ways we've navigated precarious or unstable moments in our lives—yes, our vulnerabilities, mistakes, and fears too—provides students with a real picture of human process. When students see that mistakes are part of everyone's journey, they feel more comfortable making them. When children know the paths their caregivers took, or the problem-solving they had to do to reach a given goal or milestone in life, they pave the way for continued conversation about all the ways we can be.

Encouraging caregivers to talk to their children about adversity and challenges reinforces the idea that our journeys are unique and worthy, regardless of what paths we took to get there. This honesty might resonate naturally with some caregivers, or it might feel like a tall order. Remember that every family is different. But none of us, at every juncture, have done things the "correct" way. The very nature of adversity is when things don't go according to plan and we have to improvise to come up with a new way.

We can encourage caregivers to talk to their children about times they faced doubt. Even caregivers who do this readily might not realize this has a connection to literacy when, in fact, problem-solving and discussing potential pathways toward achieving a goal *is* foundational literacy.

To support this communication with their children, we can share talking prompts with our families. For example, we might encourage them to discuss:

◈ A time you felt stuck or lacked clear direction and had to find your own way

◈ A time when you deviated from the defined pattern

◈ A time you did things differently from those around you

◈ Something that you have a unique way of doing

◈ A time when you felt the recommendations you were given in school or at work didn't suit you, your learning style, or your working style

I appreciate Britt Hawthorne's take in her book, *Raising Anti-Racist Children: A Practical Guide to Parenting* (2022). On discussing topics that might feel uncomfortable with children, she lists three questions caregivers could pose back to children that not only signal adult process but also communicate willingness to continuously learn. She reminds caregivers to face conversations readily, even if we don't know answers. When adults are unsure of how to respond to something, Britt suggests the following:

1. "We'll talk on Friday when I have more information," or

2. "What three questions do you have for me? I'll go research them," or

3. "Can you tell me what you already know?"

In my work with schools, we've also learned that when given opportunities to come in and share their personal knowledge in any area, families and caregivers report feeling more empowered to share of themselves with their children at home, too. I've heard from families that their own children were more interested in learning from them and asking questions when their peers saw them in action in class. It not only built confidence in their abilities as a caregiver, but it helped their children see what is special and interesting about their grownups.

"All of a sudden, it was like what I do for work is important," said a friend of mine, an apartment building manager, after visiting his first-grade daughter's classroom. "Then she had a lot of questions about what I do all day."

Another way we might support parents and caregivers as they elevate process at home is to show them ways to help their children problem-solve independently, especially when it comes to low-risk activities or challenges. This happens every day at my house: when Ezzy was learning to tie her shoes. When Ehsan couldn't open his paints. When Eliana struggled to navigate a social issue at school. When newborn Eloisa's arrival disturbed our quiet and intimate evening storytime. But these everyday home occurrences require some intention in navigating that ultimately supports children's understanding that there are no single solutions. Parents might find some strength in a simple two-step structure for this: identify the problem, and make a plan. We can support caregivers in this by suggesting that they:

◈ acknowledge the emotion or issue their child is facing, then prompt them toward a plan

◈ recognize with the child that there may be trial and error

◈ orchestrate and celebrate places of "safe failure" in the home

As a mother, I sometimes find it frustrating when my children don't understand that I need to be at work on time, so everyone needs to get their shoes on, even if it's hard to tie laces or wait while Ezzy figures out how to open the new nut butter lid. Sometimes, my kids get exasperated, too. I know all too well the pressures of time constraints, and I admit I am sometimes not the patient mama I endeavor to be. In my better moments, however, I slow down and try three things:

◈ **Name the observed emotion/challenge:** *I can see that you're frustrated. You've tried many times to open that zipper.*

◈ **Validate the emotion:** *That would really annoy me, too.*

◈ **Prompt a plan:** *What's another way you might do that? What options do you have? What can you try next?*

Sometimes I even think about calling on a sibling for more support, suggesting that another kid join in the troubleshooting together. After all, in the real world, we can always phone a friend. Questions like these open doors to connection and closeness between children and their caregivers while, at the same time, giving their caregivers agency and confidence to elevate the literacy principle of processing through rough patches that we encourage in the classroom every day. The following chart shares some ways we can suggest that caregivers further elevate process, in ways that connect to what you're tackling in the classroom.

# Elevating Caregiver Involvement Around Process

| If you're focusing on . . . at school . . . | Caregivers might . . . |
|---|---|
| Book choice | Share what they are reading for work or pleasure, even sometimes reading aloud parts to their children to explain what they're enjoying or confused about. I do this all the time, and my kids are used to asking me by now what I'm reading, what I don't like, and what might be next for me. |
| Reading stamina | Encourage grabbing extra time for reading between activities or events, celebrating wins, and extending the number of minutes over time. Encourage families to do their own "work"—anything they need to get done—in these windows of kid reading time, as opportunities to either read alongside children, pay bills, or handle anything that needs to be handled. |
| Peer collaboration | Orchestrate ways for children to share ideas with other kids in their home settings, by helping to set up playdates with neighbors, hangouts with cousins, or even just sibling scenarios. Perhaps caregivers can ask children to share their opinions about toys or food preferences and explain why; set kids up for drawing together, and ask questions about what they see in their friend's work. Perhaps we recommend visits to public art spaces together where kids can collaborate by talking about their curiosities and questions. |
| Summarizing what happened in a text | Name with kids what happened in a shared experience first, next, and last, or summarize what happened in a movie they watched together by naming across their fingers the order of events. Invite caregivers to share the sequence of their process around a family favorite activity such as cooking a certain food or playing a favorite game. |
| Learning genres | Encourage kids to share facts they learn or information they know about a specific topic to connect to nonfiction, and, when reading or watching a movie together, discuss what's fictional or true and how they know. |

## Inviting

Through weekly newsletters, family conferences, or face-to-face conversations, we can highlight for families common processes that feel natural and readily doable as part of the everyday fabric of their lives. Families and their children might plant seeds together in window boxes, watering them daily and watching the sprouts grow. They might plant vegetables in pots; they might visit local nature museums like Chicago's Peggy Notrebart Nature Museum to observe butterflies emerge from chrysalids over time. They might notice the changes in the belly size of a family member who is pregnant, following along with how the baby is growing over time. We might suggest an added step of drawing or jotting daily change over time, strengthening observation skills and the idea of step-by-step recording like the scientific processes we teach in classrooms. We might ask kids to narrate orally what they see happening across a time period.

The possibilities are endless: learning a dance. Building muscles. Making food. Gardening. Pottery. Mastering a video game. Lengthening meditation. We want to remind our families that the very idea of growth over time is a literacy ideal we value in our reading and writing classrooms and that this is something they already do in their homes. Perhaps the root of discomfort around process is frustration and disappointment in one's own ability to get it right. It might come from a prism of perfectionism, and it might come from a desire to tell the authority what they want to hear. It might come from a psychology of needing external validation and praise to feel successful. Either way, it's important to remember the emotional response we intrinsically have when it comes to gray area and growth over time. Every time we fail at something, however insignificant or heavy, we naturally have a response that either compels us to get up and try again or become impatient with ourselves. This is true for our children, too. In talking to friends and family about getting good at growing our ability to consistently evolve, every one of them brought up the discomfort—and fear—that comes alongside that growth. Fear is a necessary part of process.

I channel Felicia Rose Chavez, author of *The Anti-Racist Writing Workshop:* "A product-based mentality only exacerbates this suffering, due to its emphasis on a polished final outcome. With that mentality, a blank page conjures fear of failure and rejection. . . . Fear wants to exercise control, strangling the life energy from our words until they are flawless. But real writing, the pursuit of authentic voice through process, not product, is a release of control." Chavez contends that process is ultimately learning to be generous with oneself (2021).

Remembering the rawness of criticality around process is crucial when it comes to our young people and communicating this ideal to families. Nobody is meant to be perfect; nobody actually is. Getting to a place with answers and understanding includes an emotional journey too.

## Considerations for Inviting Caregivers to Elevate Process with Their Children

The state of our global culture right now breeds a sense of urgency for results. Devalues reflection. Points blameful fingers at mistakes, as opposed to celebrating mistakes as potential opportunities for innovation and growth. Part of an effort to combat these norms—both inside and outside the classroom—takes an intentional slowing down. When our children are young, like Ehsan with his Lego building, they live in process. They know nothing of results. Adults are the ones who impose stressful products and perfectionism, often without the celebration of the mess necessary along the way to get there. Caregiving deeply and lovingly requires slowing down to becoming more in tune with children and how they see the world.

There are many ways educators might make suggestions to caregivers about elevating process. Here are some ideas to get you started:

◈ Talk with your child about frustrating moments of change, narrating over emotions while describing what you felt along the way. Recognize that families may approach struggle and discomfort differently; recognize, too, that emotional responses to growth will inherently be dependent on culture, context, and background.

◈ Notice your family rituals around grief when loved ones pass. The ways that families gather to grieve together, memorialize the event, and rally around each other afterward offer natural places to communicate with children the value of process, not only in the ways we feel but also when it comes to the passing of time as process.

◈ Together, notice environmental changes, from seasons to neighborhood buildings. Track changes over time in your home, neighborhood, and community. In our house, when the kids outgrow something they've been wearing, we talk about their bodies growing and think about who might appreciate the clothes we're ready to pass on. In young children, kids can notice seasons changing as part of their cyclical nature. Paying careful attention to the leaves on a tree, for example, or the ways animals in the neighborhood behave at various times of the year is a powerful way of amplifying process in caregiver communities.

◈ Honor the reading process by reminding sibling duos and friends to read to each other, that each is learning at their own pace, and that reading

*Friends and siblings reading together honors process over time.*

pictures is a form of reading. I put up pictures of my kids reading books and leave them on the fridge so they can see which books they appreciated at different times in their lives. They tend to naturally notice—*Remember when I read the entire* Warrior *series?*—without my prompting them, signaling to me that they're noticing their own changes in reading over time.

◈ Study together the Japanese art of kintsugi, a technique in pottery repair where gold is inlaid into cracks and broken parts. Instead of trashing the broken pottery, kintsugi renders the pieces more beautiful. Caregivers might further discuss the ways beauty is created from what appears broken or ruined after reading *Beautiful Oops* by Barney Saltzberg (2010).

◈ Encourage authentic reasons to write. Kids love to make signs for doors or for welcoming visiting family members, invitations for sibling play performances, and handwritten notes to the tooth fairy or neighbors. Remind families that inventive spelling is an important way for students to grow their writing skills, and it's not necessary to overcorrect or help with every detail of these imaginative creations.

◈ Build and dismantle Legos, blocks, or any household items, reimaging new designs. My youngest likes to build using measuring cups and Tupperware while I cook. You might say, "Whoa, that is an interesting structure you built. Why did you add a window there? What if we included two doors instead of one? If a storm comes, what part would be sturdiest? Where can we strengthen the structure? What is this part for? Who lives here?" The verbal explanation behind the decisions kids make is the most important part of this suggestion.

◈ When looking at children's writing and work they've brought home, families might ask questions about the process instead of commenting on the final piece alone. Instead of commenting on the way a final presentation looks, encourage them to ask:

- How did you come up with that idea?

- What other ideas did you have that you wanted to explore or hope to study next?

- What changes did you make from the beginning to the end?

- What part are you particularly proud of, and why?

- How could you have written or composed or organized this differently?

- What part do you think could still be improved? What would you want to change if you wrote this again?

- Show me how your piece changed from your first draft to the last one.

*Two pieces of authentic writing: after a nature walk and a sign that reads, "Dear Ryan and Ryan I left art."*

Imagine the head start—and instructional promise—we could tap into as literacy teachers if our students brought in examples from their own lives where they observed, discussed, and valued authentic changes across time. They might be able to more readily write about these experiences, and they might have a ready foundation for learning as part of a journey, as opposed to a drive for finding a single answer or the one response a teacher was seeking. They might more fluently try again after missteps. And they might be more willing to take learning risks that often result in ingenuity as a result.

Elevating process as part of everyday life in addition to classroom practice is an essential component of a holistic literacy experience, one that centers children and their growth over time. When we embrace the nuances, mistakes, and multiple paths for ourselves and acknowledge that there are no single solutions or ways of doing things, we communicate to children that they, too, can be nuanced. They can achieve different goals in so many ways. They, too, can pave their own way.

# Reflecting: Process:
# The Journey Is the Learning

| What are some natural processes outside of school that your students experience? | List out some important processes in your literacy block. |
|---|---|
| | |

| Why are the processes in your literacy block important to you, and how do you communicate these values to your students and their caregivers? | How does the myth of perfectionism show up in your own life? How might sharing ways you've overcome this with students and caregivers illustrate process over product? |
|---|---|
| | |

| How does a cultural focus on perfectionism and final product keep learners from embracing the growth opportunities found in process? How might you overcome these ingrained barriers? | List your favorite projects or assignments to do with children. How can you add a celebration of process to each of these activities? |
|---|---|
| | |

# Reflection Space

Feel free to use this additional space to process the reflection questions and your own thinking from this chapter.

# Chapter 3
# The Collective: Elevating Community Through Collaboration and Inclusion

When my first daughter was a toddler, I signed her up for music classes in Chicago. I was a new mom, full of both self-doubt and energy. At music class, the kids would rock in front of the teacher, who strummed his guitar while making funny new spins on nursery rhymes like "This Old Man" and "Wheels on the Bus." Halfway through class, the teacher brought out small primary-colored carpet squares with a variety of noise-makers: a seeded shaker, a cowbell, a little drum. Kids were supposed to sit solo. The problem was, each class, Eliana would plop down on another kid's square, trying to fit her little bum beside him while playing all of his instruments. She didn't want to make music alone. Being a new mom unfamiliar with social norms around sharing space in these classes, I'd act a little exasperated and grab her, trying to keep her wiggly body on her own square. But the child who she happened to plop down beside every class came weekly with an amazing caretaker, an older woman from Belize named Laverne. One week, when carpet time came and Eliana once again scrambled over in an attempt to share the tiny carpet square and the other child's instruments, Laverne pulled out a bigger carpet square, one she had rolled and tucked in the back of a stroller. Eliana and the little boy fit comfortably side by side. This way, they could make music with all of the instruments together. And just like that, my daughter and the rest of the music class learned an important lesson in inclusion and the collective.

This chapter is centered on the pedagogical stance of elevating the collective, which means caring for and teaching each individual uniquely because we know their special contributions bring value to a larger whole. This lesson is about stepping away from individualism and competition and stepping toward collaboration, sharing, inclusion, and collective care.

## Listening

When my Amu Jalal died several years ago of complications from sickle cell disease, my dad's siblings came together from all over the world to celebrate his life and mourn. I flew from Chicago to Pittsburgh with two of my kids, baby Ezzat strapped to my body. I had expected to find a sad, dark home, full of crying amehs and devastated family, maybe even some chest pounding—the mourning norm of the women in my family back in the Middle East. But instead, I found myself marveling at the strengths of each relative's differences, not altogether discombobulated, banding together not only to support one another but to execute a small, lovely funeral in a country whose cultural traditions around passing were altogether unfamiliar.

My Ameh Roaya stood in the kitchen over multiple pots of dill rice and green stews, stirring when necessary but mostly just tending to each dish with devotion. The aroma filled me with faith. She hummed a low melody to herself, the tune of Javad Maroufi's classical Persian ballad, "Khabhaye Talaee," which my uncle had often closed his eyes and rocked to, seated in a burgundy living room armchair when he was alive. There was my cousin Sahar, just in from Brooklyn, calling mosques to determine which would work best for a visit and eulogy. My father, who had flown in from Dubai where my parents lived at the time, was calling restaurants to check on Middle Eastern catering, jotting notes for the pricing of Ali Baba's, where I used to wait tables as a teenager and summers between years at the University of Michigan. My little brother, Rami, had a role: to call friends to share burial details. My eldest ameh, Ameh Joon Shokooh, had a role: to receive visitors and accept overseas condolence calls. My Ameh Shamsi, who was closest to Amu Jalal: to cry as often as necessary. Her tears weighed enough for us all.

I expected bickering under pressure or one sibling taking over the planning. I expected an eruption over who should make a decision for what food was served or which photos were preferred to decorate the table (that job was on me). But instead, a smooth, collective spirit prevailed. I was filled with comfort in knowing my grandmother's lifework had been successful: her children, coming together, laying one to rest, holding hands, smiling through tears, nourishing one another with home-cooked goodness. In her child-rearing and deep, lifelong care for her seven children, she never pitted them against one another. Never set up competitive stances or made comparisons; never assumed each son or daughter's life had to look a certain way. One of her main refrains was faghad hamdigaro dari—you only have each other.

And so, in this moment of quiet observation in a kitchen far away from my grandmother's long gone Khorramshahr kitchen in southern Iran, I felt a surprising centering of self. Each sibling contributed with what they individually could give, and with their unique offering, a beautiful celebration unfolded: poignant, nuanced, meaningful. Personalized and just for us.

## Honoring

You might be asking: How can this family story, of one Iranian American's experience in grieving, teach us about classroom literacy practice? Places of intersection arise. Moments where I learned from life and show up better for my children as a result. In my grandmother's refusal to set up binaries of good and bad, competitive or individualistic, she set up her children to support one another. They formed a strong team through a mindset of collective care. They contributed what they knew and could do well to a more meaningful whole. I see literacy experiences and the learning journeys of our classrooms similarly—as ecosystems where not every individual must do or create the same exact thing. Rather, our tapestry as a learning community is more sturdily and uniquely woven as a result of allowing for each child's strengths, desires, and specialties to shine. Like a welcoming kilim, this partners beautifully with antiracist educator and activist educator Lorena Germán's scholarship on "textured teaching." She writes, "Our future is textured by incoming languages, blending cultures, welcomed voices, true history, robust art, all of life, warm and tasty food, and more" (2021).

But that asymmetry and texture are sometimes missing in the compliant, sanitized education spaces that so many practitioners believe are the right way classrooms and schools should look. The beauty is in the individuality, the mess, and the noise; the learning is in the missteps, failures, and attempts to get that whole collective community growing. Much of that texture depends on involving families in our processes and practices. It reminds me of the ancient Persian story my uncle used to tell, about a flock of thirty birds in search of the famed simurgh, a benevolent mythical creature roughly analogous to the western Phoenix. But when the group of birds arrived at what they believed to be the simurgh's lakeside home, what they saw was their collective reflection in the crystal water. You see, si, in Farsi, means thirty; the simurgh was not an all-powerful mystical being but a manifestation of the awesome power inherent in the flock.

We can honor these cultural stances as educators by recognizing the strength in our students' varied and imperfect uniquenesses. Because that is exactly it: our power resides in our collective strength. We are what we are seeking.

## Connecting

Exalting each child's uniqueness to support the whole community shows up in strong literacy classroom teaching regularly. When we heterogeneously group our students because of their various strengths and needs, we are tapping into this foundational teaching ideal. Though each one of our students excels in their own ways, they contribute meaningfully to the entire group's work in a reciprocal manner. Everyone's voices and ways of being are necessary.

Likewise, no caregiver is without expertise, whether something they get paid to do for a living, something they enjoy doing for fun, or something that was passed down by ancestors. When students see that families and learning come in all sorts of configurations and everyone has a unique outlook or way of living, especially when showcased by their teachers, they see uniqueness as an asset for their classroom communities as well. This is a literacy ideal we want to communicate: no two people are the same, nor should they be. It's joyful collectivity and the weaving of a larger, more beautiful whole community that we aim to cultivate.

How can we further communicate this in the classroom? One way is by consistently saying with our words and our actions that there is no one way to do *anything*. Standardized methods of assessing children in a capitalistic society set students in competition with one another. Our grading and assessment systems compare students, grouping them with labels like "high," "middle," and "low" that undermine what students *do* know and *accomplish well*. We might not be able to fully dismantle national assessment practices, or push every day against schoolwide mandates for tracking students. But if we can learn anything from my grandmother, it's that each individual contributes *what* they can *when* they can. Each contribution is a gift.

When we consider what it means to create change at school, our minds often go to the widespread historical or social change that we read about in books. When considering our own capacity to make institutional impact, people often say, "I could never make that kind of a difference. I'm not the president, or the governor, or a member of the school board . . . I'm just me." When considering our own classrooms, it's important to remember that YOU are the most impactful change agent. You might not make the widespread policy, but you make the daily choices that define the school experience for children and families. This is not the positional power associated with someone with an executive title; rather, this communal power comes from being most consistently proximate to children and families.

This power allows a practitioner to decide: your displays, your celebrations, your discipline policies, your seating arrangements. You get to decide your classroom culture, your grading methodologies, how recess goes, and how you communicate. Filter these through a lens of collectivism and you'll realize the enormity of your impact.

We can construct opportunities for student contribution, collaboration, and discussion in ways that celebrate uniqueness instead of attempting to create rote replications of a single result. If we imagine the literacy classroom like an orchestra, where each individual plays a different instrument but their collective contribution crescendos to a magical whole, we begin to see the dynamic and important uniqueness of each participating member.

What does a collective spirit mean for how we teach literacy? Put simply, it means that in the classroom we are fostering collaboration over competition, identifying ways that each child's strengths contribute to the community. It means avoiding binary thinking, which assumes a "this or that" framing that lacks nuance. It means incorporating the talents and treasures surrounding our students in their homes and communities to cultivate a deeply layered learning experience, tapping into a rich funnel of caregiver expertise and learning that also comes from every child's lived experiences.

> When considering our own classrooms, it's important to remember that YOU are the most impactful change agent. You might not make the widespread policy, but you make the daily choices that define the school experience for children and families.

For example, we can refrain from setting up classroom and schoolwide competitions when it comes to reading, because those systems establish hierarchies of winners and losers. Reading joy needs to be at the heart of our work as literacy educators. When we celebrate writers and craft ways for students to share their different thinking based on what each individual needs, we are communicating that individuality within a collective is possible. When we read aloud books with varied characters who all think, look, and act differently—and then facilitate discussions of how important it is to celebrate all of our differences, instead of creating divisions because of them—we are communicating with children the myriad ways that people live and learn. All valid. All different. All necessary as contributions to a textured whole (society, school, classroom community). There are no single ways to be.

As I write this, book banning is happening all over the United States. People are creating divisive laws to keep stories about people—mainly Black, Brown, LGBTQAI+, folks who have been historically marginalized, underrepresented, and silenced—out of curricula and out of the hands of children. These attempts keep regular-life stories away from children, which skews reality and misrepresents the world. This concerted effort not only tries to wipe out people's histories and experiences but also is simply untruthful and dangerous. It will take all of our unified and persistent efforts to continuously share whole and entire histories and stories of ALL people. We must be sure that families and children see themselves in their learning and have the opportunity to learn about others.

## WE ARE NOT ALL THE SAME, NOR DO WE NEED TO BE

America as a "melting pot" is a myth. This belief assumes we all melt into one version of "American"—a national "normal" to which we all aspire. This is simply not true. The idea of a melting pot erases everything unique about its constituent members.

In its own understated way, this expectation extends to school. Children infer the message that school often implies: to be successful here, you need to be one kind of American. One kind of student. One kind of learner. And in America, though we've never named it out loud, that kind of American often refers to white and middle class. That one kind of student often refers to obedience. And that one kind of learner often refers to "neurotypical." The assumption that success looks only one way is harmful. It is damaging to children. This way of doing school has forced students and caregivers to contort themselves to fit that mold, and anyone who can fit it is labeled successful and given all the benefits that come with that label. And anyone who can't fit that mold is labeled unsuccessful or "different."

This idea reinforces itself because young people feel the weight of these labels, even when no one names them out loud, so they comply. Some rebel, and the children who do are those who are most often marginalized in school. Caregivers see this and, in their desire

**WE ARE NOT ALL THE SAME, NOR DO WE NEED TO BE** *(continued)*

for their children to be "successful," often preach compliance and assimilation. We can disrupt this harmful narrative by helping caregivers see all the different ways that success can look and by supporting children as they work toward the vision of success that they want most for themselves.

I suggest reading widely about teaching students of all backgrounds, including: Erica Buchanan-Rivera's *Identity-Affirming Classrooms: Spaces that Center Humanity* (2022), Don Vu's *Life, Literacy, and the Pursuit of Happiness: Supporting Our Immigrant and Refugee Children Through the Power of Reading* (2021), and Jung Kim and Betina Hsieh's *The Racialized Experiences of Asian American Teachers in the US: Applications of Asian Critical Race Theory to Resist Marginalization* (2022).

## Celebrating Alternative Ways of Doing Things

Our teaching language can be powerful. When we name our teaching points as just one way of trying a reading or writing strategy, we communicate that each student can make the decision that best suits their literacy work, based on their own toolkit of strategies—and there are lots of ways. It took me years to learn the potential impact of adding two simple words to the start of my teaching points. Instead of saying, "Today I want to teach you that personal narrative writers brainstorm by . . .," I revised it to say, "Today I want to teach you that *one way* personal narrative writers revise is . . ." I remember when one little boy at a school in Chicago's Jefferson Park asked, "But Ms. Q, what are the *other* ways?" After all, readers and writers in the real world don't follow a single path to reading and writing in the exact same ways. When we think about authentic teaching that will serve students beyond the classroom, we must be cognizant of how we portray literacy strategies. Matthew Salesses, author of *Craft in the Real World*, speaks on revision and feedback in a real writing workshop like this: "Possibilities for revision might take the form of suggestions, but would be better as what-ifs (e.g., what if this evil character had a really nice friend?) and should focus on process—things to *try*" (2021). What if our young people learned just like this?

It doesn't end with direct instruction. During independent practice, we might make room for students to choose: which editing strategy will you try today? We cultivate space for reflection: Which attempt felt most useful? What might you try next? We remix ideas from our peers: Did your table partner experiment with a different way you'd like to try next? We remember that we are teaching not only literacy strategies but metacognitive flexibility in what students want to try, and why. This diversification of teaching language and teaching practice paves the way for access and for sharing uniqueness among us. As classroom teachers, it isn't our job to dictate and direct but instead to facilitate and share examples so that students can try, fail, and try again, learning which decisions work best for them.

Similarly, every single assignment need not be a collection of individual content-knowledge demonstrations but more about giving learners ample opportunities to contribute to a larger whole, so they can see their work come to fruition in what amounts to something larger than what they could've pulled off alone. It's no wonder that the collective spirit and camaraderie of a school play or the success of a team sport is infectious; it's that very specific stronger-together mentality we hope to cultivate. I believe if we become more attuned to a collective contribution mindset, our students will better support one another and ultimately feel more capable of applying themselves outside of the classroom. Beyond that, an ethic of collective care and collaborative learning is a core underpinning of culturally nourishing teaching for *all* children. Gloria Ladson-Billings, widely known as the mother of culturally relevant teaching, writes, "To solidify the social relationships in their classes, the teachers encouraged the students to learn collaboratively, teach each other, and be responsible for the academic success of others. . . . The teachers used this ethos of reciprocity and mutuality to insist that one person's success was the success of all and one person's failure was the failure of all" (2021).

As you continue to reflect on highlighting classroom connections through a collectivist mentality, consider how you might adopt or adapt the following starter list of possible practices to elevate your own classroom practices:

◈ **Building discussion towers,** to which students add a block or a manipulative of some kind as they participate in a conversation at their tables, so they can see a visual and tangible representation of their collective discourse. This practice allows children to see that their individual voices are adding to a larger whole.

◈ **Collaborative art projects,** in which each child is tasked with adding to a big art piece, whether envisioning a scene from a novel on big butcher paper or adding cut-outs to a collage to depict interesting details from an article. When many people's contributions are added to a single piece of paper, there's something more beautiful about the end product.

◈ **Suggesting roles** to students in book club discussions, while asking for one shared group artifact to demonstrate learning at the end of a week instead of individual, replicated worksheets for each child to fill in.

◈ **Creating talk paper chains** for individual contributions like sentence starters that scaffold comprehension, such as *first/next/then*; *this makes me think . . .*; *this part helped me predict . . .*; *I wonder if . . .*; and so on. I've done this as well with synonym chains to support the elevation of various mundane words like *good*, *bad*, and *mad*. When kids see a physical manifestation of their collaborative thinking, it's powerfully tangible.

◈ **Collaborating with peers** to create a simple Google Jamboard or paper poster after paired reading experiences—for example, sharing about book characters with one student illustrating how they envision the character, another inserting evidence from the text to support their depictions, and then working together to orally explain how characters changed over time in a voice recording.

◈ **Revisiting the charts** we've coconstructed with students in past lessons over and over to determine whether they continue to warrant a semi-permanent place in the classroom. In the same vein, we can invite students to share the work of creating additional classroom charts as necessary to elevate the collective needs and strengths of the learning community.

◈ **Coconstructing classroom norms** around the ways we want our environment and our community to look, sound, and feel. You can pave ways for students to contribute meaningfully to decisions around where chairs go, how the library is organized, and how to decorate the walls. Students can notice and decide whether things need to change based on their own needs. One of my fifth-grade Chicago communities gathered in a morning meeting to decide as a group what to do about wiggly after-recess bodies. They decided that they needed flexible seating options for independent work time. That power in group decisions supported more engaged readers and writers.

◈ **Differentiating between equity and equality** by explaining with care that what's fair isn't giving everyone the same exact classroom support but instead ensuring each child gets what they need. For example, not all four of my children get the exact same experiences, items, or even time with adults, if I'm being honest. But each child gets what they *need* at any given time, to the best of our abilities, whether that's a special after-school cookie date with Mama for Ezzy, because I recognize she needs to unpack a big feeling or setting up Ehsan with a weekly FaceTime session with his friend Luke back in Chicago, because it's clear he's missing his close camaraderie with friends since our move.

# More Ways to Explore the Power of the Collective

Sharing learning experiences together while exploring a variety of resources will always be one of the best ways families can support the power of the collective. Here are a few favorites to keep the conversation going with kids, caretakers, and educators.

| Text Title | Author |
| --- | --- |
| *Zero* (2010) | Kathyrn Otoshi |
| *This Is a School* (2022) | John Schu<br>Illustrated by Veronica Miller Jamison |
| *Come and Join Us: 18 Holidays Celebrated All Year Long* (2023) | Liz Kleinrock<br>Illustrated by Chaaya Prabhat |
| *The Boy with Flowers in His Hair* (2022) | Jarvis |
| *Can We Please Give the Police Department to the Grandmothers?* (2023) | Junauda Petrus<br>Illustrated by Kristen Uroda |
| *Essential Labor: Mothering as Social Change* (2022) | Angela Garbes |

## Celebrating Differences in Strengths

Communicating a stance of collective importance given each person's individual strengths may or may not be relatable to caregivers. My kids bicker, but they know they'll hear mama say, "There is no one way," in response to at least half of their gripes about each other. Though this mindset might be different from what most adults learned in education spaces themselves, we know now that students can and should celebrate their variety of individual approaches to the same end. Still, caregivers may not be thinking in this frame when it comes to school. There is no one way to write a book response. There is no one way to revise a writing piece. There is no one way to achieve a final result. Though some families believe this adamantly, there is no specific way academic pathways are supposed to look. There are no prescribed, single journey approaches. We have to find ways to communicate that. When we focus our energy on these individualized ideals and their arbitrary constructs, we often end up leaning on didactic and rote thinking that doesn't serve the community collective. Unfortunately, this mindset is often ingrained in our school culture. I'll never forget my first grader being distressed that I was suggesting she design her poster for a social studies project about recycling in a landscape format. Her teacher's example showed a vertical design, so Ezzy wouldn't believe me when I said she could turn hers horizontally. Our children learn to do what they believe is the *only one way* quite young. But we can purposefully push against this.

Caregivers may need further clarification on how holistic literacy practitioners organize their classroom communities and make purposeful instructional design decisions that exalt this collective stance (see Figure 3.1). For instance, when we thoughtfully layer a multitude of diverse, multimodal texts (songs, art, videos, audio, alphabetic texts) that share a broad scope of people, places, and ways of being, we ensure students are exposed to myriad ways to tackle either the same thematic subject or learn more widely and deeply about a given culture (Muhammad 2020) while advancing the literacy ideal that there are so many ways to be. But communicating with families about the thought and purposes that went into the selection of layering texts is also important. We can turn to so many groups and organizations to support this work. Your town librarian is a valuable resource, as are organizations like We Need Diverse Books or Pen America, which have materials for communicating with caregivers.

> **Our children learn to do what they believe is the *only one way* quite young. But we can purposefully push against this.**

Because caregivers may have been introduced to single stories, such as the whole-class novel, or because they may not have had experience with multimodal approaches to reading and writing, it is critical we communicate the reasons we advocate for far-reaching and expansive definitions of what we consider viable texts. We must share with them the importance we place on using a wide array of texts to enhance students' understanding of any given theme, topic, or group. When we explain our criteria for this work, such as the considerations for curating that follow, and how they communicate to children the unique and important contribution of individuals, we minimize confusion and contradict erroneous assumptions. We don't have any specific right or wrong ways of being. Whole groups of people cannot be represented by a single text alone. All texts are not created equal. When caregivers understand this rationale, they know better what we are trying to accomplish in the classroom and may even consider some of these questions when selecting texts with their kids, too.

◈ Contributions

- ◆ Who wrote the books?

- ◆ What perspectives do they offer?

- ◆ Whose perspective of this same content is missing, or would we want to seek?

◈ Achievements

- ◆ Do the texts showcase a diversity of experience in all areas: socioeconomic, gender and sexuality, ethnic, racial, cultural, and so forth?

- ◆ Are we celebrating all kinds of people, along with their customs, joy, and ways of being, instead of solely presenting the strife and hardship of BIPOC groups during single calendar months?

◈ Currency

- ◆ Has the text been published recently?

- ◆ Does it represent the latest thinking around a topic?

- ◆ Does it represent the reality of what happened, without omitting facts and parts of history?

- ◆ To what extent does it portray people living in today's world, highlighting a variety of experiences?

Caregivers might be surprised to know that one way to ensure we are exposing students to the most up-to-date thinking and historically accurate information is by updating our text collections. Powerful literacy teachers are always looking for texts that accurately depict the world and fully represent the people in it. The role of a holistic literacy teacher focused on collective care includes the communication of these important considerations to caregivers, too.

**FIGURE 3.1**

*Collective-Focused Literacy Instruction to Clarify with Caregivers*

| Literacy Instructional Practice | What Might Not Be Clear to Caregivers |
|---|---|
| The structure of groups and group work includes ways for all students to share and add value; student roles don't always have to be the same. | Each child plays a unique role in a group project, and not all students need to submit the exact same artifact or final product. This might look different from what caregivers are used to; it might feel like a surprise that their child is the "note-taker" or "designer" as opposed to the sole creator of the entire project. |
| Not all students receive the exact same assignment during independent work time; rather, teachers make suggestions for student artifact creation that is tailored to their needs and strengths. | When students are allowed to apply their own reading and writing strategies to their compositions or independent reading books, their responses and writing output might look different. In a well-oiled workshop classroom, students might receive different small-group minilessons. One group might learn about pop-out words for dialogue, whereas another might learn about elevating mundane verbs. That means their writing output might look dissimilar, and there is beauty in that. All students are growing and learning on their own trajectories. |
| Facilitating student application of strategies to multiple texts instead of learning through whole-class novels alone. | We are more able to showcase multiple perspectives and share learning across varied voices when we teach in strategy-based ways that allow for students to see a plethora of angles and ideas. What's more, students learn collective ways of being that contribute to a community when they share, instead of everyone having the same answers to questions connected to a single book. |
| Student growth is often determined based on where the child began and not necessarily compared to peers in the class. | Grade-level standards for where students "should" be when it comes to reading and writing measurements are social constructs. A strong, holistic literacy practitioner will grow children from wherever they enter our classrooms, avoiding labels like "high" and "low," which purport an assumption of where students "should" be at any given moment. Although we have standardized testing metrics to adhere to, many other forms of data are available to us to share the learning journey and celebrate the child's growth. |

*(continued)*

FIGURE 3.1 *(continued)*

| Literacy Instructional Practice | What Might Not Be Clear to Caregivers |
| --- | --- |
| Allowing space for multiple strategies toward an outcome. | We are careful when naming teaching points in lessons and conferring, to showcase that there's more than *just one way*. During independent practice, students are encouraged to choose: which reading strategy will you try today? Which move helped you understand the text better? Caregivers may need to hear that, as holistic literacy teachers, we aren't telling students what to do but teaching a variety of strategies for how to communicate something, then allowing them to make their own choices on how to accomplish it. |
| Cultivating environments where assignments can (and should) look varied. | When we send work for our students to complete at home, we have to be careful they know there is no one way to complete it. When we insist that assignments are completed in one specific way, we are reducing children's capacity to think for themselves and sending the erroneous message that all work, pathways, and presentations are the same. What's more, caregivers often feel stuck and unable to help their children because they, too, believe there's only one right way. We need to communicate that supporting children with their literacy learning can take many different forms. |

## Elevating

Students can learn from the wisdom of so many different people in their communities—in religious spaces, from neighbors, local business owners, sports team coaches, their grownup's coworkers, to extended family members across the globe. When I interviewed author Sabaa Tahir for We Need Diverse Books, about her young adult novel *All My Rage* (2022), she emphasized the importance of the cool and relatable imam who leads the mosque. She wanted for Noor, the teenage protagonist, to deeply trust someone outside of her family, because that's what's true: we are shaped and supported by all sorts of people in our lives. In fact, it's often the broader village that grows us the most. During the pandemic, my best friend Ryan's partner, Ryan, moved into a studio apartment above our garage, so my children grew up with two dear Ryans as invaluable parts of their village. But my story is not unique. Every child has chosen family that is truly critical to their upbringing and shaping of the future.

## Reenvisioning Family Trees as Community Maps

No doubt, you're familiar with the traditional family tree project. My own kids come home with these year after year, a stenciled outline that they need to fill in with great-grandparents, grandparents, parents, and siblings. For my children, being raised in a two-parent household with strong connections to both sets of grandparents, this has been a fine project that goes fairly smoothly in each instance. A few phone calls to Mama Mahnaz and Abuelo get them the names of family members from Iran and Puerto Rico that they need. But as we know, all families are different. These family tree projects have the potential to be both frustrating for students and alienating to their caregivers. When I spoke with longtime educator and school leader Nefertari Nkenge, she shared such an example of frustration about her daughter's experience, particularly around a "normed expectation of who lives in the house."

"It would have just been Mom and her. But she made it about 12 brothers and sisters, and that made me grin. The teacher interrogated her and made her feel some kind of way. Jendayi considered her godsiblings who spend the night; I'm Mama Nefertari to all these children; my daughter calls their mothers Aunties— so she's listing names. The teacher says, these are your siblings? The teacher just couldn't understand."

A more inclusive and culturally sustaining approach would replace these experiences of othering and frustration. Nefertari contended: "Our family experiences—verbal tradition as an African people—it's not something that's going to be captured in a paper-and-pencil family tree. Nor is the respect we give our non-blood relatives, many of whom are elders we learn from. It would never get the depth of what I shared now, or what my daughter understood in the third grade. To visualize and draw illustrations of experiences with this large family—even though it's just the two of us—it needs the narrative for us. For Black and Brown people, for you to see the depth of what we're describing . . . in the end, I wanted to communicate: see how rich the narrative is in who we are? That is never captured in literacy assignments in schools, nor is it captured in the ways we give credence to it in our own traditional way."

Black, Brown, and Indigenous communities, especially, have longstanding and deep understandings of the importance of the collective and, furthermore, the far-reaching relational ties that shape knowledge of ourselves and who we are. Indigenous scholar Shelbi Nahwilet Meissner (2022) writes, "*Kinship*, as conceived of by Indigenous scholars, does not refer merely to heteronuclear families or biological relatives (TallBear 2018; Whyte 2021). Rather, 'kinship' is used to

*Community map examples from a classroom in Chicago's West Lawn neighborhood.*

describe the relationships between all entities that share responsibilities for one another." And also, "Indigenous conceptions of kinship expand beyond Western conceptions of family and include relationships among humans, non-humans, animals, plants, and spirits—these relationships inform Indigenous knowledge systems." We can learn from these deeply rooted ways of being. If we are to honor all families and their ways of being, we must design curricular activities with collective inclusivity in mind.

I imagine the objective of the original family tree exercise was never to fill in box after box in rote fashion but to foster curiosity among children and conversation with their elders around history, connection, and contribution. An alternative that acknowledges a more nuanced reality of family structures, while, at the same time, speaking to a broader collective behind every child, would be a free-form community map, taking the same concept of illustrating connections between the child and those who have an impact on their lives, while still eliciting conversation between the students and adults around the history of connections. Community maps can thoughtfully tease out a literacy ideal we all appreciate, weaving a textured tapestry of unique individuals with myriad experiences toward a greater collective that is inherently beautiful *because* of its nuances.

Some people who have played an enormous role in raising me would never have shown up on a traditional family tree graphic organizer. Amu Hamid, with his ceaseless guidance, unending support, and unconditional love, wouldn't have had a place on a simple stencil, because he was my father's sister's husband. But the reality is, he was one of the people who raised me. I was one of his daughters. He piloted my daily decision making with compassion, care, and experience. If I were a student able to design the outline of my adult community, he would've shown up as the family giant.

To get started with community map projects, you might offer students and their caregivers an open-ended set of ideas along with a few quick parameters and find this is plenty to inspire a variety of individual products. Leaving the process open allows for families to cocreate and coimagine with their children. And, when they share their final projects, I often marvel at folks' oohing and ahhing, which almost always results in an even greater degree of imaginative iterating and dreaming of interesting projects further down the line. I generally make the following suggestions and leave the rest to them:

◈ Visually represent the people in your collective who support you.

◈ You're welcome to use a tree form to guide you, but feel free to diverge from that template to represent your loved ones in the way that makes most sense to you.

◈ Draw connections between the people in your life using visuals.

Just as my Amu Hamid had superhero-like individual strengths that contributed to our family collective as a whole, as students and their caregivers work on this project, invite them to highlight how different individuals have made them stronger together with prompts like:

◈ Who is this person to me?

◈ What makes them unique?

◈ What talents do they bring to our family/group/community?

◈ How does having them with us bring us closer and make us stronger?

◈ What might our collective look like if we were missing this person's contributions?

◈ How did our loved ones who have passed contribute meaning to our family? How did they shape us? How might we keep their legacies alive? How do we ensure their memories are a continued blessing?

Dream big here. Read aloud from books where families look different (see the periodically updated document linked to the **QR** code provided for a suggested roundup). Prompt children to share with peers before brainstorming on paper. In one second-grade Chicago classroom, students discarded the tree image altogether and, instead, talked about who grows in their hearts after their teacher

*Suggested Titles for Inclusive Family Stories*

mentioned all the different contributors to her garden: bees, flowers, weeds, birds. All of those elements contribute to and nurture the garden's vibrancy, just like all of the people in our hearts.

These community maps can even be coconstructed with caregivers or orchestrated as a collaborative family project in schools, which is particularly impactful with siblings in multiple grades. They can begin on family literacy nights and end in a cumulative showcase, or they can be smaller-scale and more personal in nature. Either way, the conversations that ensue as a result of creating community maps are invaluable representations of a literacy ideal that ultimately frames much of what we aim to accomplish as teachers.

## Getting to Know Individuals to Inform the Collective

Each child has strengths, challenges, and uniquenesses that affect the way they operate in the classroom. When we shift our attention away from where each child is *supposed* to be and appreciate instead the nuances of each, we elevate a collaborative philosophy of strength. As a mother of four young children, I feel certain that I know their needs better than anyone else. I can tell you what will send my Ezzy into hysterics and what will ignite Ehsan to work. Their father knows precisely what to say to our eldest, Eliana, that will propel her into full-on protective sibling mode, and we know what topics interest each of them individually. And because they are children, these things change often. If we make it part of the fabric of our classrooms to more readily incorporate the inherent insider knowledge families and caregivers have about their children, we will be more equipped to design our instruction according to what fuels them and simultaneously remind families and caregivers how critical it is to reflect on these sorts of questions at home, too.

It is our responsibility as classroom educators to deeply know what our students bring with them. Children are not blank slates. Rather, they bring with them a plethora of rich experiences that make them the gorgeously textured children they are. Many of us send surveys to families and caregivers with simple questions asking what their student's challenges and strengths are, and if there are any glaring issues we should know. You likely do something similar at the start of a new academic year. This felt particularly critical during the pandemic, when remote learning launches of a new school year didn't allow us to build relationships with our students in traditional ways. I have found that when we invite parents and caregivers to teach us about their children directly, the nuances they share support our instructional planning and strengthen families with the knowledge they already hold about their children. It is also helpful to do this critical work *beyond* the start of an academic year, sending out follow-up surveys as frequently as once a quarter or trimester to ensure that everyone stays updated as inevitable growth and change occur. Make it part of your regular conversations with families. What else might you add to the list of potential questions below?

**FIGURE 3.2**
*Questions to Ask Families and Caregivers That Celebrate Individuality*

- What does your child do particularly well?
- What are your child's interests? How does your child learn about the things they love?
- What motivates your child? What is your child excited about?
- What makes your child smile?
- How does your child best demonstrate their understanding of something?
- How does your child operate independently at home—with siblings, for mealtimes, for everyday activities like getting dressed and getting ready for bed?
- Who is your child particularly close to in the family or in friendships?
- What is your child uninterested in, if anything, and what challenges arise at home as a result?
- What does your child do when they are unhappy with a situation or if something unexpectedly changes? What does your child do when they're frustrated?
- Have you found any specific tactics that work especially well in communicating with your child?
- How has your child changed recently?

When we ask caregivers these questions, they sense our desire for a greater understanding to serve the whole child. This genuine interest paves the way for stronger relationships and establishes an initial and obvious assumption that families know their kids best. It symbiotically elevates the importance of reflection and deep listening, all in pursuit of serving the children in front of us most lovingly. These surveys reframe the way we approach individuals in the classroom— as one part of the unique fabric of the community.

A note about surveys being sent home to families, either as Google Forms or paper documents: if these forms of communication elicit low response rates, find other ways to connect. Reduce barriers. Don't forget to translate into home languages for all families who might benefit from communicating in a language other than English, whenever possible. At the start of relationship-building with new families and new caregivers, ask their preferred mode of communication and connection.

You might set up a booth at a back-to-school or curriculum night for families to sign up and connect with you individually; you might have open office hours twice a week after school for an hour as you're doing classroom work for families to stop in and confer; you might ensure an extra touchpoint with families at a time when they're required to visit the school for materials pickup. My friend Kate's son Theo attends a charter school in Brooklyn where families are invited into the classroom on the first Friday of each month. Teachers I support in Los Angeles like to send home quick video clips of themselves explaining a literacy tenet and then they show it again to families when there's an in-school opportunity. It takes time and repetition to communicate inclusively and clearly. Either way, it is critical we continue to establish and maintain lines of honest communication with all student caregivers, regardless of family makeup (see Chapter 1).

# Elevating Caregiver Involvement Around the Collective

| If you're focusing on . . . at school . . . | Caregivers might . . . |
|---|---|
| Group projects and working in teams | Encourage their children to play team sports or work in teams to get a job done at home, like cleaning up or packing for a trip. They might play board games in teams. |
| | Group projects show students that each person has an important role to play in a collective and shared effort at accomplishing something together. Although caregivers might think group projects are just something we throw into the curriculum as an option, when they realize that working in groups is part of our methodology in exalting a stance of community mindset, they're more likely to think through that angle at home, too. |

ELEVATING CAREGIVER INVOLVEMENT AROUND THE COLLECTIVE *(continued)*

| If you're focusing on . . . at school . . . | Caregivers might . . . |
| --- | --- |
| Taking responsibility | Give kids responsibilities at home: clearing their plates, feeding a pet, keeping library books in one place near the door for return. They might have responsibilities to care for a younger sibling or be part of the food preparation—like lunch making or keeping a list of missing ingredients for a recipe.<br><br>Like with students in the classroom having responsibilities to take care of the classroom library, the class pet, or class materials and supplies, caregivers can lean into the idea that sharing responsibility for aspects of the community provides space for open conversation about caring for our collective together. |
| Shared reading | Share reading of all kinds with their students on a regular basis. Night-time stories shouldn't be a privilege or a punishment to be taken away. Caregivers might playfully change voice levels and change their body language in shared reading, similar to how educators do in the classroom. |
| Putting on a class event or performance | Encourage imaginative play at home that results in putting on a performance—like my own kids and their fashion shows or restaurant openings. They can involve children in annual traditions that include students in various roles. What we learn about students' differences and uniquenesses in these occasions is rife with teachable moments and understandings that help us further exalt the collective. |

## Inviting

Another layer of this work can take the form of suggesting to families and caregivers the power of collaborative projects at home, ones that allow multiple family or community members to contribute. Of course, all families will approach these suggestions differently based on their available time and resources. Offer examples without judgment and provision when you can with supplies from your school. We always invite Ryan and Ryan to join us in backyard projects where everyone has a collective hand in adding to the creation. For example, they'll bring the paints and we'll bring the paper and spread out on our back deck to piece together something pretty to hang on our refrigerators, or plant tomato and cucumber seeds in the hopes that something will grow. One winter we cut snowflakes together from shiny paper, creating a complete window installation for the holidays.

As with all rich learning experiences, growth happens when teaching is woven, connected, and collaborative. Caregiver literacy is no different. Family literacy includes an integrated approach on the part of school leaders and educators that doesn't feel compartmentalized, separate, or one-size-fits-all. And because families are as diverse and unique as the children in our care, grounding our methodology, curricular design, *and* communication in nourishing, collective care is essential. That means exalting experiences for students that show a wide range of pathways and end results, consistently touting a community effort and embrace, and thoughtfully reimagining assignments or literacy tasks that alienate and exclude.

**As with all rich learning experiences, growth happens when teaching is woven, connected, and collaborative. Caregiver literacy is no different. Family literacy includes an integrated approach on the part of school leaders and educators that doesn't feel compartmentalized, separate, or one-size-fits-all.**

## Considerations for Inviting Caregivers to Elevate the Power of the Collective with Their Children

We can make suggestions to families and caregivers for collaborative projects that elevate the contributions of each individual. As always, recognize that no two families are alike, so our suggestions might feel foreign or unhelpful to some, while resonating perfectly with others. Here are some recommendations families might want to try or that you can incorporate during a family literacy labsite (read more about family labsites in the conclusion, on page 163):

*Collaborative mandala making with items at home.*

◈ **Create circular nature mandalas** together out of leaves, rocks, and sticks, with each family member collecting and adding to the project. You might snap a photo and make a digital or physical bulletin board of these, or you might discuss the ephemeral and short-lasting nature of things, even in intricate and meticulously executed projects. I marvel alongside my children at the sand mandalas created all over the world, and we talk about how patient and process-oriented their creators must be. We discuss how each individual's contributions lead to a greater whole.

◈ **Construct collaborative paper weavings**—cut strips of newspaper, construction paper, or magazines and weave them together to form a flat table covering. My daughter loves making these with her little sister because they feel so proud to have created something our family needs: placemats for each family member's plate.

◈ **Engage in large-scale painting projects** by rolling out cheap butcher paper or long white rolls of paper across the floor, taping the paper down, and getting out all kinds of art supplies to collaboratively paint. Play music and just go wild alongside your child. I highly recommend getting big and messy; there's something refreshing about not caring what the final result is meant to be. I firmly believe that kids having the chance to play with materials alongside grownups lays the groundwork for discussion or contentment to just be together. Talk about who added what and why that was an awesome contribution. Notice how your child contributes to the project. How do they behave alongside siblings who joined in? Could you invite neighbors and other community collaborators?

*Engaging in large-scale collaborative art elevates collective strength in cocreating.*

◈ **Organize a space** in the home together, like the garage or a closet, coming up with a plan for how to make the space more inviting, user-friendly, or easy to manage. My kids *love* to organize closets with me—not joking—because they help come up with systems that work better when they see a space *not* being utilized well. The other day my eldest was complaining about what we call the junk drawer in the kitchen, saying that it had become a catch-all for everything from Legos to bills to keys to Ziploc bags. I asked if she had a better solution, and she helped by labeling little bins and announcing all disparate items would be returned to their rightful places once weekly. This seems silly, but she gave the role of returning the items to her little sister, who felt proud to play a part.

◈ **Plan together to plant a garden**, whether on a windowsill, in a pot, or in an outdoor space. Research together what kind of light a space gets and what sorts of seeds might flourish as a result. Allow for each child to contribute their thinking, add to the plan, and then execute it, planting the seeds in the soil together. Invite siblings to sort out how they'll share the work of tending to the seeds by watering and observing any growth.

◈ **Write letters or cards together.** I might be the last person on Earth who loves to send snail mail, but it's a joy for me to receive cards in the mail and an even greater joy to send letters in the mail. Not all families or children might enjoy or find relevance in this activity, but two of my children have gotten into it with me. It still feels collaborative because we address and stamp the cards together and then walk to the mailbox to deliver them, and we even melt a wax candle seal to close each envelope. The kids need me to light a flame to burn the candle down, and they often ask my opinion when it comes to colors and designs. Either way, it's a simple and collaborative caregiver-and-me activity that has the added benefit of being literacy rich.

*Role-taking for family pet care.*

◈ **Care for a family pet** collaboratively by thinking through a plan together for feeding, walking, or cleaning schedules. My friend Jake has elaborate family plans for the caretaking of the fish and its tank; they've named the fish Carnage and the Green Brothers. Each son is responsible for a day of feeding and a once-monthly tank wash-out. To hear his wife tell it, "There's a whole ritual behind going to the fish store, picking out the fish, and replenishing after fish deaths. And don't forget the shrimp and little frogs." Each family member plays a role.

◈ **Play collaborative games** like charades or board games meant for collectively achieving a goal, like *OutFoxed* or *Hoot Owl Hoot*. Carefully select games that don't necessarily set up competitive binaries with winners or losers but support an ethos of teamwork toward success and fun together.

When we reimagine the ways that our literacy classrooms look to expound upon a multidirectional partnership with caregivers—both in communicating literacy tenets of the importance of the collective and in representing those beliefs when we teach—we tap into the instructional promise our students already bring with them when they first step foot in our classrooms.

# Reflecting: The Collective: Elevating Community Through Collaboration and Inclusion

| Where in students' lives do we naturally see differences and individual uniqueness? | How might you communicate the importance of the collective to students in your community? |
|---|---|
| | |

| What suggestions might you make to families to exalt the ways individuals contribute to the collective whole? | How can you connect student home and community experiences (of contribution to a greater collective) *in* the classroom? |
|---|---|
| | |

| How might you remix your existing curricula, texts, or assignments to exalt the collective uniquenesses of varied experiences? | What suggestions might you give caregivers that highlight uniquenesses in their personal stories with their children? |
|---|---|
| | |

## Reflection Space

Feel free to use this additional space to process the reflection
questions and your own thinking from this chapter.

# Chapter 4
# Observational Literacy: Reading the World

I grew up in a predominantly Jewish community in the Squirrel Hill neighborhood of Pittsburgh. The families of my classmates were mostly upper middle class and wealthy, tight knit and culturally not too dissimilar from my own. My best friends had beautiful rugs, though they weren't from Iran. They had traditions around adolescence and grieving that felt like our own. Though my friend's families lit candles for Shabbat on Fridays and usually had a mezuzah above their door frames, I felt comfortable in their spaces. Perhaps this is because of the longstanding similarities between Middle Eastern traditions or because I was well versed in code-switching and showing up in ways that made me most palatable and similar to those around me. I remember going to my friend's houses and sliding naturally into conversation with their parents, who were usually doctors or lawyers. I would update them on the goings on in my own home while omitting parts I thought might be embarrassing—no honest discussion of the dysfunctional nature of our relatives' visits; no admitting anything that

would make me seem too different. In hindsight, it was my first lesson in the painful nature of assimilation. I role-played into the version of "appropriate" that I thought would put me in the best position to climb social ladders. I read the world around me. I understood who was privileged in it, and I contorted my identity and mannerisms to mirror theirs. By doing this, I gained some things. I may have lost some too.

This chapter's pedagogical stance recognizes the complicated nature of reading the world and transferring those skills to classroom practice. Young people come to us with so much. They know what it means when their teacher sighs in frustration. They know what it means when a sibling slams a door or when a parent gives "the look." Like I did, kids know how to read the world for power. That they derive meaning from wordless occurrences *is* reading, and many kids are skilled at it *before* they ever enter a classroom. Much of this organic knowing is scrubbed from them when school communicates the message that reading is only book stuff.

## Listening

There's a little girl with one long braid peering over the counter at the salon, watching silently as customers move in and out of the glass storefront. Her brown eyes are large. She's observant, like her mother, who she has accompanied to this space for years.

"Eyebrows," says one woman when she enters, slipping her phone in her bag.

"Arm wax," says another, coming in right behind her.

Bollywood tunes play on the speakers. The rustling of paper can be heard from the back rooms, as beds are switched and prepared for the next visitor.

The little girl, entering kindergarten in a few weeks at a charter school in Brooklyn, leads the way down the short corridor for the waxing client but signals the chairs to the first with a wave of her arm. "Threading's over here," she tells the woman, encouraging her to sit with a flick of her wrist.

I continue to watch as people from the street come in and out of the salon. One person comes in asking for money. The little girl shakes her head repeatedly and respectfully until he lets himself out. Another comes in asking whether they do eyelash extensions, and the little girl—after looking at her mother and asking a question in Hindi—responds in English to the client, "Come back Thursday."

I overhear the woman in the back, who continues to FaceTime a man named Richie throughout her entire service, cracking jokes that the little girl in the front giggles at. I think she's translating for her mother.

Though this scene takes place on a sticky August afternoon in the Bedford Stuyvesant neighborhood of Brooklyn, hundreds, if not thousands, of students in the United States experience similar moments with their caregivers on any given day. The salon—and barbershop—is the bedrock of many Brown and Black communities. It is a vibrant, intergenerational space where witty banter can be heard and social cues are read, where young people learn to navigate conversation and questions. They learn the power of observation. And it is in countless life spaces like these that our students glean critical literacy skills that we as teachers can encourage and transfer to alphabetic reading in the classroom.

Literacy does not solely exist on the pages of a book. Literacy is tied to our identity and to place. To force a single version of literacy is to force a single version of humanity.

## Honoring

What can this child's experience tell us? She was learning, alongside her caregiver, how to closely read people. She was learning empathy. She was learning the art of listening, translanguaging—using the full repertoire of her language skills—and conversation. Our children read their environments and interactions between people all day, every day. They lovingly analyze the facial expressions of their family members, leaning in to determine whether their grandmother's back hurts today or whether their little sisters are fussy. They learn to know how wide a space to give folks on a subway platform; they learn how to interact with people in offices and stores.

> Literacy does not solely exist on the pages of a book. Literacy is tied to our identity and to place. To force a single version of literacy is to force a single version of humanity.

Research shows that children react positively or negatively to the facial expressions—or lack thereof—of their caregivers. Babies reach more readily for toys when their caregivers' faces show interest and engagement, but they'll proceed with caution if their caregivers' facial expressions reveal fear (Lawrence, Campbell, and Skuse 2015). Children have an innate ability to read expressions, particularly of those who they rely on for survival. This is a form of reading. It is observational literacy, which involves reading the world, reading visual images, reading experiences, reading situations, reading environments, and then inferring meaning and backing up that thinking as a result. This skill is critically important not only when it comes to alphabetic literacy but also when it comes to life-long literacy practices that will serve our children far beyond classroom walls.

Children have countless opportunities to observe their caregivers interacting with the world around them, from grocery store behavior to religious communities to family reunions to navigating new and unexpected adventures together. But one of the most common—and one I have found to offer easy access paired with high impact—are those universal stories and experiences highlighted daily in kitchens across every home in the world. In my work with schools across the country, I've explored with teachers how these "kitchen table" experiences might be elevated to build strong home-school connections.

These stanzas in Clint Smith's poem "Tradition," from his collection *Above Ground* (2023) perfectly depict the literacy learning that happens in the rituals of meal-making of caregivers alongside children:

> On Sundays we make French toast
> the way my father made French toast
> with me. Each of you stand on stools
>
> that lift your bodies above the counter
> and I roll your pajama sleeves up
> to your elbows then ask you
>
> if you're ready to start. You both take turns
> shouting out everything we need to begin—
> an incantation of ingredients that have become
>
> the lyrics to a song only we know. So much
> of what I try to do as a father is put back together
> the puzzle pieces of what my father did for me.

In my own home, my mother, aunts, and grandmothers cooking in the kitchen is chief among my earliest memories, not only because I learned how to prepare food alongside them but because I deduced their personalities, relationships, and histories by reading their behaviors and movements. I learned to infer from my observation the power dynamics in my family and how the pressure of Iranian culture dictates some of that navigation. As a child, I would sit on the counter and watch them toss meticulously chopped ingredients in big pots to feed our family and anyone who would stop by; Iranian cousins, neighbors, and all kinds of visitors were always welcomed. There was no measuring. There was often debate. "We don't make it that sweet in the south," Ameh Shamsi would tell my mother of the fesenjan recipe, a stew made with walnuts and pomegranate molasses. "In Khorramshahr, we make it tart."

My mother would step back. She always quieted in those microinteractions, becoming more demure. My aunt was ten years older, and, thus, she wielded power and respect.

Now, as an adult, I call my family on FaceTime to get these recipes right. "About the amount of your hand, Nawal," my mother says, and I laugh because my hand is much bigger than hers. I call her an hour later, when she berates me for not stirring it enough. "You'll burn the bottom of the pot that way," she chastises. "You're not making tahdig here." My mother is more assertive without my aunt.

The power of observation and the analysis that those observations might lead to are strong literacy practices that our students navigate naturally. With a little intentionality, we can build a bridge for those skills in our class-

*Children learn valuable observational literacy skills during mealtimes.*

rooms. What I was doing as a young child was ultimately character analysis and constructing my understanding of identity and relationships. We can support our students by encouraging experiences and suggesting questions caregivers can ask in authentic contexts at home, in their neighborhoods, and in their communities.

## Connecting

Caregivers might not easily recognize the invaluable observational literacy skills that the little girl in the salon—and every child like her who fluidly navigates social situations—is developing. Those observational literacy skills translate to an invaluable critical thinking muscle that perhaps caregivers don't recognize as important. How can we teach from this relatable place of strength, to joyfully lead engaging literacy lessons for our young students? If we believe that the teaching of literacy is actually the teaching of what it means to be human, how do we keep humanity at the center of our instruction? This question has tentacles reaching into every corner of our instructional design and decision making. With observational literacy, we can move the dial toward a more human-centered approach, one that caregivers might readily understand and that educators can build from for instructional promise (see Figure 4.1 on page 108).

## Reading Art and Pictures for Meaning

Once, when I was reading aloud to Ezzy, she became flustered.

"Go back and read that page again," she demanded. I did, thinking this was yet another instance of Ezzy asserting herself.

"No, read it again! You're not saying it right," she said, this time raising her voice.

I was confused. I wasn't skipping any words. I was reading a simple picture book verbatim. I sighed, trying once more.

"You didn't say that it's *storming*," she asserted. I paused to figure out what she meant. The pages in the picture book depicted a dark cloud with pouring rain, but the words made no mention of a change in the weather.

What she was exhibiting is one of the earliest stages of literacy development, one that we can call out for parents, in addition to letters, sounds, and blending those together to make words: making inferences about text from supportive images is a form of reading. In fact, Ezzy's perception that the words on the page didn't match what she was reading in the image is a critical thinking skill that literacy teachers absolutely aim to cultivate. We must communicate with caregivers that opportunities exist to engage our children in rich observational literacies all around us, drawing a connection between the critical thinking we aim to cultivate in all of our children's experiences.

> If we believe that the teaching of literacy is actually the teaching of what it means to be human, how do we keep humanity at the center of our instruction?

Caregivers want to know that it is essential we provide rich opportunities for students to grow their reading lives in a variety of ways. As Jan Burkins and Kari Yates write in *Shifting the Balance: 6 Ways to Bring the Science of Reading to the Balanced Literacy Classroom*, "Given the way the brain reads, the complexities of our alphabetic system, and the amount of practice students need to learn to read, it is worth mustering the courage to look for opportunities to better leverage phonics instruction. After all, one important purpose of phonics instruction is to develop the brain's orthographic processing system, bringing letters, sounds, meaning, and context together" (2021).

In a workshop approach to teaching literacy, after a succinct and digestible minilesson, teachers send students off to independently read and write, to practice strategies in their ever-growing toolkits. Teachers in the youngest grades might ask students to snuggle up and get cozy with a book, regardless of whether the child is already reading alphabetic text. I've heard parents say, "Oh, I'm pretty sure she just memorized that book," when that isn't necessarily a bad thing. In fact, the comfort of a repeatedly read, potentially memorized book is akin to the nuzzle of a baby blanket, offering a pattern and a knowing that builds confidence in the child. My own kids memorized Leslie Patricelli's *Yummy Yucky* and *Quiet Loud*—approximating the story via familiarity and image—before they learned to decode alphabetically. This happens all the time.

Teachers and school leaders need to message to caregivers unfamiliar with our work that reading pictures *is* emergent reading—just like recognizing vowel sounds is—and it is absolutely part of the foundation of literacy. I'm not saying this is where we stop: of course our kids need to go on and receive explicit instruction in foundational skills so they can learn how to decode/encode words and be able to read and express their thoughts—but leveraging our innate observational skills to support our attempts to make meaning, both from images in front of us or drawn across our imaginations from the text—inferring—is a skill we teach across all grade levels. We can share with caregivers that the literacy skills connected to analyzing an image mimic the skills necessary to analyze texts, and when kids have these early experiences celebrated, they

*Caregivers often reread favorite stories.*

are better equipped to learn fluidly in the classroom. The same is true for composing writing, as students in a writing workshop, for example, create narratives from images, nonfiction pieces out of infographics, or storyboards and companion books to accompany their learning (Coppola 2019). All of these classroom endeavors are built on the foundational experiences of analyzing and observing the world around them with some degree of criticality.

It is important, too, for students of all ages (and their caregivers) to know that reading does not solely mean decoding words and reading alphabetically. We know that wordless picture books tell beautiful, intricate stories. We know that artists tell stories with their creations. When we set up students to read the world with the same criticality lenses we apply to alphabetic text, we empower them to turn those tools to everything in their lives. And for students with various reading abilities, who may not have the confidence to discuss alphabetic text with their peers, reading something they can see with their eyes evens the playing field. All kids can look, see, ask questions, and discuss, thus boosting their confidence overall.

We have a responsibility to connect our children with the world in ways they find interesting and resonant with their realities, which, oftentimes, means drawing directly from their social realities. "Children often disengage from learning because the texts we give them don't speak to their lives, including their cultural identities, interests, histories, and experiences. They may find the texts to be meaningless or irrelevant to their lives," writes Gholdy Muhammad in *Unearthing Joy* (2023). When we bring visuals into the curriculum as additional text for reading and learning, we share creative ways of communicating the histories and stories more broadly. We can leverage opportunities for observational literacy to elevate social literacies that, in the end, are more engaging and culturally sustaining for kids of all kinds.

## Incorporating Observational Skills in the Classroom

*A periodically updated Padlet provides the perfect opportunity to showcase and share a growing collection of works from contemporary artists.*

We incorporate these observational skills into the classroom in plenty of ways. In some of the schools I support, we introduce a piece of art once weekly as the mentor text and ask that kids apply the reading strategy to visuals alone. In others, art may be selected during independent reading, and students become accustomed to discussing visuals and the decisions their creators made alongside alphabetic text. I created a roundup of contemporary artists for my students to choose from and discuss with their peers (link included through the QR code provided), prompting them with simple sentence starters like "I see," "I notice," and "I wonder." You might add, "I feel" to underscore the emotionality of reading art. They can take this further and even write what they believe the artist was trying to achieve. I often ask the question, *What story is this artist trying to tell? And how do you know?* These questions support continued analytical skills and the building of an argument with evidence from the text. A sample reproducible response form can be found in Appendix A.

One of my favorite paintings to analyze with students is one by Kerry James Marshall titled *School of Beauty, School of Culture*, which depicts a robust and dynamic salon of women not dissimilar to the space I described earlier in the chapter. Students who fluidly read social context can transfer their observation and critical thinking skills to reading art, thus growing their analytical thinking muscles. When children engage in a back and forth about the art, this dialogic approach can strengthen their conversations about books. Other artists I have loved thinking about alongside students include Bisa Butler's vibrant textile portraits, Tatyana Fazlalizadeh's murals, or Ekua Holmes's bright street scenes. All of these artists are activists and storytellers in their own rights, and using their creations as text opens the doors to authentic and engaged learning for all ages.

As students grow accustomed to having conversations and reading art, we apply these same questioning stems to alphabetic text, so they can see connections between reading the world and reading in a book. They notice they're making the very same moves. Students discover for themselves that this is not just art; this is the beginning of reading and thinking deeply about books.

School of Beauty, School of Culture, *Kerry James Marshall*

# See/Notice/Wonder Art Analysis Chart

A reproducible response form can be found in Appendix A.

| Sample Questioning Prompts | Sample Elementary Conversation | Sample Middle Grades Conversation |
|---|---|---|
| What do you see? | I see a lot of women.<br>I see some doing their hair or getting their hair done.<br>I see little kids and lights. | I see women, maybe dancing—it seems like movement. Maybe there's music playing.<br>I see there are people of all ages. |
| What do you notice? | I notice they are dancing. | I notice it feels like a fun place. It feels engaging and warm because of the bright colors. |
| What do you wonder? | I wonder what is on the ground. | I wonder what the little kid is peering at in the front. |

# More Ways to Explore the Power of Observational Literacy

Sharing learning experiences together while exploring a variety of resources will always be one of the best ways families can support the power of observational literacy. Here are a few favorites to keep the conversation going with kids, caretakers, and educators.

| Text Title | Author |
|---|---|
| *Platanos Are Love* (2023) | Alyssa Reynoso-Morris<br>Illustrated by Mariyah Rahman |
| *I'll Go and Come Back* (2022) | Rajani LaRocca<br>Illustrated by Sara Palacios |
| *Sari-Sari Summers* (2023) | Lynnor Bontigao |
| *Cool. Awkward. Black.* (2023) | Stories edited by Karen Strong |
| *Everything Sad Is Untrue* (2020) | Daniel Nayeri |
| *How a Korean Stew Connected Me with My Mom* video text (The New Yorker, 2019) | Bryan Washington |

**FIGURE 4.1**

*Observational Literacy-Focused Instruction to Clarify with Caregivers*

| Literacy Classroom Practice | What Might Not Be Clear to Caregivers |
|---|---|
| Working in groups and pairs for projects or literacy tasks | When students interact with their peers, they learn invaluable skills how not only to navigate social situations and interpersonal behaviors but also to absorb how others think, digest information, and create differently. They're learning how to read group dynamics, which is important, too. |
| Listening to read-alouds | Listening to read-alouds prompts students to hear fluid reading in addition to offering space for them to envision the setting and what the characters look like or the information being presented. This version of listening to read-alouds can be likened too to auditory storytelling and audio books, further exalting the multimodality of reading. |

**FIGURE 4.1** *(continued)*

| Literacy Classroom Practice | What Might Not Be Clear to Caregivers |
|---|---|
| Field trips, cultural fairs, and schoolwide celebrations | Observational literacy opportunities, when students leave the building and interact with grade levels other than their own, supports learning beyond classroom walls. I always think about Clint Smith's *How the Word Is Passed* (2021), a gorgeous adult book that essentially highlights the important learning that can happen in open-air spaces. Smith writes about his visits to former plantations, the legacy of slavery, and the rich history that could be learned by students who visit. |
| Author visits or special classroom guests like surprise readers | Similarly, caregivers might not realize the rich learning that occurs when authors and new adults visit the classroom space. Opportunities for students to interact with new voices and especially people who offer insight into new layers of meaning cannot be underestimated. It is in those moments of "reading" people that real instruction occurs. |
| Assignments to interview others, whether inside or outside of the school building | When students ask questions and learn about the way other people think, act, and live, they learn new ways of being themselves. I went to school for journalism and was a newspaper reporter for years. Though I was not taught explicitly how to quickly pivot from personality to personality or situation to situation, I did gain a ton of experience in speaking to all kinds of people. I was forced to read rooms, situations, and spaces in ways that would be an incredible asset for all of our students, too. In those reporting and interviewing experiences, I learned how to read the world. |
| Notebook walks | Notebook walks allow for students to observe and create as a result of the world around them. If you're teaching a writing workshop, you might be doing this with your class by prompting notebook walks as part of an assignment. Caregivers will want to know that a keen eye on the world around us is a beautiful springboard for storytelling, questioning, and writing. When we read our environments, we are more readily able to mine for ideas. Furthermore, drawing a map of a special place or your neighborhood and thinking about moments of emotion that happened in those spaces are among some of my favorite writing brainstorming lessons. But writers will need observational literacy skills to start. |

*(continued)*

FIGURE 4.1 *(continued)*

| Literacy Classroom Practice | What Might Not Be Clear to Caregivers |
| --- | --- |
| Interacting in a workshop model | I am very transparent with students about how the workshop model goes. I share with students (and caregivers) that minilessons are a time to gather and learn a strategy that they can then apply to their own independent practice. I clarify that conferences, writing groups, and sharing sessions give students opportunities to interact with their teacher and peers, listening in on how others process their thinking, getting ideas to grow their own, and enhancing observational literacy skills—ones that support fluid navigation of world experiences outside of the literacy workshop, too. |

## Elevating

Ofelia's house is nondescript. Low, ranch style, on the southwest side of Chicago; brick, not too many windows. The curtains are almost always closed, as she appreciates a quiet calm of muted colors without exceeding brightness. She keeps her house immaculate. The aroma of sopa comes hand in hand with this house, too: pozole, albóndigas, spicy menudo rojo. In the afternoons, after teaching eighth grade all day, I would quickly gather up my notebooks, snag a book off the classroom library shelf, and sit in this very same kitchen to read and nurse, first baby Eliana and then Ehsan, grateful my babies survived yet another day without the bottle, which they had always refused.

*Ofelia cares for Ehsan.*

Ofelia's kitchen, like in many households, is the hub of her home, where she, her husband, three of her six children, and one of her grandchildren live. They meander in and out, speaking solely Spanish, lifting lids on the stove and grabbing my babies for a quick cuddle and kiss. "¿Cómo estás? Mamá Navalle," they'd say, drawing out the ending syllable while smiling at me, knowing I'd stay an hour to debrief Ofelia on my day.

One of Ofelia's daughters, Jadi, was born in the 1980s. She's the manager at a big grocery store in the city, and she was fifteen years old when she moved to Chicago from Mexico.

"At first we were really scared because we came to a place we didn't know and I didn't have the language." Jadi shared. "The school was huge. There was one teacher from Puerto Rico who was really nice, and my history teacher was Mexican. So, my mom mostly talked to the teachers who could speak Spanish, because what else could she do? She didn't know how to help."

I asked her about school and her parents' relationship to it, and all she had to say was this: "My cousins who lived here helped us with school because my parents didn't understand the homework."

But I will never forget that she ended our conversation with: "You know, outside of school, my mother taught us everything."

By offering simple, everyday observations, through her presence alone, Ofelia taught her girls to make those layered sopas. She taught me to make guacamole in the blender—smooth, not chunky and easily heaped on a tortilla chip, how *her* mother made it. She taught my kids to drink from a cup, skipping sippies entirely, as well as some conversational Spanish, a dozen nursery rhymes, and how to tie their shoes. She taught her children to save up for the items they wanted: brand new white Reeboks for the start of a school year, a firmer mattress. She kept her babysitting cash in a special spot that she'd revisit with her granddaughter, count, then return. And Ofelia taught her children the importance of community, because there wasn't a single family occasion we attended that didn't include a dozen uncles, even more cousins, joyous music and dancing. We were always welcomed as part of the family.

I've been thinking a lot about how Ofelia never felt part of the academic equation. She didn't believe she could help her kids with schoolwork, nor did she feel equipped to support them in any troubleshooting. She asked clarifying questions of the Spanish-speaking teachers, but her involvement with her kids' school-centered education stopped there.

How can we as educators highlight Ofelia's meaningful contribution while directly translating it to the confidence of her kids in an academic setting? What if we communicate more clearly with families that observing everyday practices builds strong literacy skills? How could Ofelia support classroom literacy work with a little intentionality, by perhaps asking more questions or narrating aloud the steps she was taking to accomplish a given task?

## Food Stories

One place to start with families is in the kitchen and in food rituals. Not only is the kitchen the heart of the home across many cultures, it is also a place where caregivers are comfortable—even accustomed—to modeling and teaching. It can be a place of safety, where our students' matriarchs and patriarchs exude confidence with each stir of the pot; where mistakes are embraced, laughed at, and folded into the recipe as if they were always intended to be there. And if we think about the nourishment, sustenance in both conversation and nutrients, and familial feelings of care that come from this universal kitchen table, we might even aim to transfer those sentiments to the classroom, mirroring the feelings and observational skills we want to evoke in our students' learning experiences.

Because at these tables, and in these kitchens, our families are also conferring foundational literacy skills in the course of their everyday meal-making, passing down family recipes, and sharing stories of their days, memories, and experiences. Even when we consider how many contemporary meal traditions are interrupted by busy schedules or limited access to food, the way that families come together to problem-solve food insecurity or to acquire what they need in politically architected food deserts is bold and radical literacy work. Our families don't always think of everyday life as literacy, or as a direct bridge to supporting their students in school. It is our role as educators to make this connection.

When I design culturally nourishing literacy units alongside teachers, we often start by immersing ourselves in food stories. We read all sorts of texts about mealtimes and nostalgia (see the QR code provided). We share memories connected to both sad and happy food experiences, maybe even ones of shame, like in Amy Tan's short text titled *Fish Cheeks* (a 1987 one-page narrative essay) or Andrea Wang's picture book, *Watercress* (2021). We listen to poet Joy Harjo's recording, *Perhaps the World Ends Here*, and talk about moments of learning at our own kitchen tables. During these units, we can encourage families to do the same: mining the world for food stories, talking about family recipes, and learning about family traditions about food. Inevitably, we recognize that pain and difficulty sometimes also happen at the kitchen table: that food insecurity exists, that people's relationships with food are varied, dynamic, and even fraught with emotion.

*A roundup of culturally nourishing texts to immerse students in food stories can be found at this periodically updated link.*

## Incorporating Culinary Traditions in the Classroom

The process of designing a classroom reading and writing unit around culinary traditions and food preparation can be as robust or simple as you like and will invariably extend beyond observational skills into specific reading and writing opportunities that showcase home interactions and celebrations. I've offered this through everything from month-long projects to more simple, two-week mini-units. Students might compose:

◈ Visuals (stories in image or art alone)

◈ Recipes (step-by-step)

◈ Memories or vignettes in the shape of small moments

◈ Poetry

◈ Projects in any genre

Any option you choose presents opportunities for bringing families into the instructional recipe, whether that be through initial interviews, at-home activities, or collaborative meal-making. These learning experiences are limited only by your and your students' imaginations. They can be designed for writers to make their own picture books. Students might create drawings with food parables or nonfiction content around the history and origin of specific traditions. In hybrid-genre informational texts, students research and share about the cultural background of their food stories for context. I love the way Winsome Bingham talks about her personal connection to making baked macaroni and cheese with her grandmother in the author's note of her dynamic picture book, *Soul Food Sunday* (2021), whose illustrations by Bronx-based artist C.G. Esperanza merit equal analysis, too. What's fun is inviting families into sharing their own memories and storytelling connected to the kitchen.

Our youngest students can write how-to books and list steps for recipes after interviewing caregivers; our older students can add nuance and detail to the experience of cooking alongside caregivers or sharing a meal with family. You can invite caregivers into the school to share in a potluck; you can celebrate with a class recipe compilation. One of my classrooms followed the history of foods like grits and frybread as modes of resistance and connection to family legacy, researching systemic racism in food systems, and interviewing elders for stories about cultural connections to the past. Another class studied the varied ways different cultures use rice, potatoes and bread—staples across the globe.

To fuel some specific observations and transfer thinking from home to school and back, we ask students and caregivers to consider the following questions together:

◈ What traditions does your family have around food?

◈ What recipes have been passed down across generations?

◈ What is your favorite meal? How do you prepare it?

◈ What does this meal mean to you?

◈ What memories do you associate with this meal?

◈ Who taught you how to make this meal?

◈ Where does this meal or recipe originate?

◈ What questions do you have about this meal?

# Elevating Caregiver Involvement Around Observational Literacy

| If you're focusing on . . . at school . . . | Caregivers might . . . |
| --- | --- |
| Determining importance in a text | Share their own stories and determine the importance in those conversations alongside students. For example, if we ask students to share a recipe origin story (or the passing down of the recipe, or any family story), discussing what remained at the forefront of the conversation or what shifted based on a person's geography or experience will support student understanding of importance. They might notice how different family members' retelling of a story includes different details, showing how the reader's personal experience can affect what is deemed important. Caregivers will want to know that the transference back and forth of these observational literacy skills to alphabetic text and back into conversation builds critical thinking as they engage with their children. |
| Identifying literary elements such as hyperbole, metaphors, personification, simile, and alliteration | Understand that observational literacy skills in everyday life, like the reciting of a rhyme, song, prayer, and talk—and ensuing discussion about facial expressions, hand gestures, and emphasis of the words—help students better understand the meaning and emotions evoked in the writing. |
| Sequence and transition words | Verbalize instructions for preparing a snack or meal, emphasizing the importance of sequence through transition words. Have students observe a caregiver getting ready for the day or something special. Caregivers can talk through a video game a child is playing, asking questions about how they know which order to do things to achieve success. |
| Making inferences | Use clues about their surroundings to determine where people are headed when families are commuting to school, no matter whether that's on the subway, by car, or by bus. They can look at city art, murals, and graffiti to make inferences about the intention or the reasoning for the location. Be cognizant to share with caregivers the difference between assuming and inferring, because this could be a place where bias shows up. |

## Inviting

As you continue this work you'll find so many powerful connections between observations made in the home and kitchen and the idea of learners reading the world. Observational literacy is not, of course, relegated to kitchen spaces and food rituals alone. Children learn about the world through observations at their churches, synagogues, and mosques; taking walks in their communities; and at the mechanic or grocery stores. When we travel as a family to visit friends on a road trip, I marvel at how much my children are observing and absorbing—and how many learning conversations stem from those observations alone. Some of the best conversations, stemming from the most inquisitive curiosities, arise from subway experiences. My kids ask about advertisements or geography, prices of things, or changes in environment. When we're at the park, my son wonders aloud how two ice cream trucks parked right beside each other can possibly compete, propelling us into a conversation about prices and product quality. I hope analysis and hypercuriosity is never quashed. And it's this very same inquisitive, observational stance that I know caregivers can—and already often do—engage in with their children.

By moving beyond school-focused activities and making the relationships between home and school explicit in conversations with caregivers, we can further support our literacy tenet of reading the world. We can encourage the use of authentic speech, weaving naturally between languages without compartmentalizing. For instance, back in the kitchen, we might propose that caregivers:

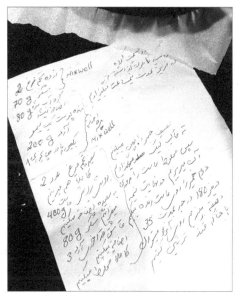

*Qarooni family recipe, written in Farsi.*

- ◈ name across their fingers, step by step, how they prepare a meal, so that children can more readily explain the process in an oral recording or story told back in the classroom.

- ◈ write out recipes alongside their children, in any language, then translate that recipe into a grocery list while identifying stores in their communities that carry each meal-specific item.

*Children learn valuable skills by grocery shopping and observing kitchen scenes.*

❖ invite children to join them on the shopping trip, armed with the grocery list, and match ingredients to items on the shelves. Older children might be sent shopping alone, especially city kids accustomed to bodega stopovers after school. All children can then describe the meal planning and shopping experience in classroom writing when back at school.

❖ talk about how recipes are passed down and what foods are meaningful or special to them, and why.

Whether it's special occasions or just everyday meals, families and caregivers already have foundations in place to support observational learning and inter-actions with others. And it is in harnessing the excitement around these special times together through expensive literacy experiences that we can create more nourishing caregiver collaborations and speak to multiple layers of the work we're trying to accomplish.

## Considerations for Inviting Caregivers to Elevate Observational Literacy with Their Children

Beyond kitchens and meals, families can enhance observational literacy in several ways. And if caregivers have zero time at all, like so many of us, we can simply communicate the literacy ideal that reading the world matters. A simple and fun move I often do with my youngest is to ask questions about how people in illustrations or situations and images must be feeling, specifically pointing out how we must know. Here are a few more possibilities:

◈ **Tell stories** across book pages by noting interesting points aloud while building a cumulative summary, "It seems like she's feeling . . ." and "Now he's going to . . ."

◈ **Read aloud** wordless picture books, narrating with kids what they think might be happening. Among our favorites are: *Another* by Christian Robinson (2019), *Door* by Jihyeon Lee (2018), and *Wallpaper* by Thao Lam (2018).

◈ **Ask questions** as you move through your community, talk about what's going on around you, share what you wonder, and make inferences. You might ask: what do you notice? What is changing? Why do you think it looks that way? Who do you think paid for it? Who benefits from that? Who is left out?

◈ **Watch TV, movies, and sports** together, asking: What was that part about? What just happened? How did the characters or people feel? How did you feel when you were watching it? What do you predict might happen next? When watching basketball or soccer, invite conversation around team decisions and dynamics.

The truth is, our students are learning powerful observational literacy skills alongside their caregivers in their regular lives, every day. If we honor and elevate the analytical skills they are building outside of the classroom in our literacy practice, we will be able to position caregivers in a space of strength. We will connect students to their classroom literacy learning with more confidence and relatable, authentic practice. And, we'll easily be able to share with families how they can continue to grow their children's literacy skills with these natural, holistic ways of communicating.

# Reflecting: Observational Literacy: Reading the World

| | |
|---|---|
| What observational literacy skills do you know your students already engage in and fluidly do well? | List five students, and think about their family and home lives. Specifically name the ways they navigate the world outside of the classroom with strength. What do those observational literacy skills tell you about each student? |
| | |
| In what ways might you incorporate visual literacies into your classroom text analysis (e.g., by reading art once a week, by adding wordless picture books, by including images as conversation connections during independent reading)? | How will you communicate with caregivers that reading the world *is* strong literacy practice, with transferable skills to alphabetic text? |
| | |
| Think about your own culturally nourishing food stories. What memories do you have in the kitchen or at the kitchen table that you can share with your students as examples of reading the world in your home? | What suggestions might you give caregivers that elevate their children's everyday talk and observational literacy skills in the kitchen or home, bringing confidence and those stories to support classroom practice? |
| | |

# Reflection Space

Feel free to use this additional space to process the reflection questions and your own thinking from this chapter.

# Chapter 5
# Talk: The Power of Oral Conversation to Grow Ideas and Connect Us

I peeked into my daughters' shared room and smiled at my mother, who was curled up on the pink kilim. She was telling the girls stories before they fell asleep. There was no book in her hand. She was describing a scene in Iran when she and her siblings were young, saying that she sewed everyone's clothes. Eloisa interrupted to clarify: "You *made* your clothes?" My mom laughed and said yes, she liked to hand-sew for her sister, Afi.

Peering into this scene through a mother's eyes afforded me the distance to understand how important these nighttime stories are—and were for me as a child. Unlike my parents, I was born in the United States. The first time that I remember going to Iran, I was eleven years old. I smelled the air and saw the mountains and experienced the sounds all around me. All these things were familiar to me because of my parents' stories. They did not know that they were doing so, but they had been building a map for me, one that had been years in the making. Stories are road maps to the future.

Oral storytelling builds similar pathways for kids. Story by story, these internal road maps help them make sense of the world: to understand its customs and idiosyncrasies, its experiences and mysteries, and its tragedies and triumphs. I knew the world of my parents because they told me its stories. Because of my mother's oral storytelling, my children would have the same.

In this chapter, we'll explore all the ways that speaking is connected to powerful learning. In school, this is an important pedagogical stance to strengthen. Some of us have grown far too comfortable with certain students speaking often and others speaking barely at all. And many of us, perhaps due to overwork and exhaustion, often limit our classroom discourse to "raise your hand if you have the answer." Because so much of learning is tied to experience and speech, this inequity of dialogue becomes an inequity of opportunity. This does not have to be the case. Instead, we can capitalize on the speech patterns, topics, experiences, and stories from home that students bring with them.

## Listening

My mother was 22 when she had me, still in college outside Pittsburgh. Having recently emigrated to the United States from Shiraz, Iran, near the dusty Zagros mountains where amber-hued persimmons grow plentifully, she was navigating multiple new worlds, from young motherhood to studying in a new language, to missing her parents and siblings, with whom she was very close. She transported me around campus on the back of a burgundy bicycle, begging friends to watch me so she could attend class.

In the evenings, she read two books to me on repeat, and I originally thought it was because I loved them, but now I know it's because that's all we had. When she wasn't reading these two books, falling asleep midsentence, she told stories from her head: long, drawn out, in Farsi, like a melody. She filled me with stories of juicy pomegranate plucking in their backyard, packing creamy dill-jammed salad olivieh pitas for rides out of the city with Baba Ghambar and Maman Ezzat to Persepolis to see the ruins of Darius the Great's ancient empire. She would tell me about meeting my gregarious uncle for the first time at the college's student union and how he introduced her to his brother-in-law, my father; how tall, dark, and handsome he was; how surprised she was to meet her match, another Iranian, clear across the world. When they fell in love, my father would write notes to her in scrawling lettering—backwards, so she would be forced to decipher them with a mirror.

The stories my mother told me are among my most cherished childhood moments and an incredible testament to the power of storytelling, which felt like sustenance in my formative years. I sometimes can't tell where my mother's memories end and mine begin, and although I was born and raised in Pittsburgh, I feel I know Shiraz intimately. Did these stories, solidified in my head as my own memories, shape my understanding of language? Absolutely. Did they engender a love of words, which, stitched together in narrative, transported a young American-born girl to a land she had never seen halfway across the globe? Definitely, yes. Did the fact that they were not spoken in English impair their power to build community and convey history? Of course not. These are many of our goals as literacy educators. The power of oral storytelling and rich conversations, which already exist in so many of our students' homes, is precisely what we aim to exalt in the holistic literacy classroom.

## Honoring

When my father describes his most meaningful moments from childhood, they always involve storytelling: running with excitement as youngsters to the family radio after lunch to listen to the ongoing oral saga that aired live at noon. Sitting at the feet of Bibi, his grandmother, as she recited memorized fairy tales about knights' sword fights and royal love from the Persian *Shahnameh.*

Healer and Indigenous scholar Robin Wall Kimmerer, author of *Braiding Sweetgrass* (2013), writes about the power of passing down stories through generations, even when they're taken out of context or altered slightly, akin to a game of Telephone. She writes, "But, even when it is misunderstood, there is power in the telling." Stories, like compasses, provide orientations with which we can make sense of the world.

I've marveled at the ways children and families communicate and build conversation, whether or not we as educators see those interactions and recognize their ripples in classroom conversations among students and their peers. When my friend Acasia and her son, River, visited from Chicago, he excitedly told me about the Black and Jewish summer camp he attended. I love River, so I really wanted to hear him. He said that he appreciated that all the counselors looked like him, animatedly describing his favorites. Acasia pulled me to the side to say that River is actually "painfully shy" in the classroom, usually reticent with other adults. "You always seem to really want to know," Acacia said. "You ask questions. You're genuinely interested." That compassionate listening stance that consistently invites safe space for a child isn't something we learn from a teacher program. Questioning and listening in conversation and talk building

> **Stories, like compasses, provide orientations with which we can make sense of the world.**

is something care-centered teachers do every day. For someone to really want to *hear* your thoughts, they must *inquire* before rushing in with their own opinions or commentary. This demonstrates care, and it is where learning and reflection often happen. All good conversations include purposeful listening moves, too.

When I think about my most revered relationships, they are almost always grounded in talk. With my closest circle and best friends, there's the regular updating on what we've experienced recently, from big life occurrences to the mundane—what we ate, who we saw, what we did. There's telling funny stories about things my family missed. There's capturing the banter of my children and sharing that back with my parents so that they can laugh about moments that pass too quickly. There's gleaning wisdom from great-aunts and -uncles, or my teacher mentor, Marv Hoffman. There's problem-solving together. There's communicating idioms to our loved ones that are not quite translatable in English, like del be del rah dare, which means "our hearts have telepathy" or "we were thinking of each other at the very same time." All caretakers and families have rich opportunities for inquisitive, authentic conversation with one another just by living everyday life, but it is our responsibility to communicate this ideal.

> For someone to really want to *hear* your thoughts, they must *inquire* before rushing in with their own opinions or commentary. This demonstrates care, and it is where learning and reflection often happen. All good conversations include purposeful listening moves, too.

As a teacher and caregiver myself, I've learned that children will open up and discuss more with me when I pull back first from my own agenda. There is a time to impart knowledge and build thoughts together, but I've noticed a pattern in most children: the more we gently listen and notice, repeating back what we think we heard, the more apt children are to volley in a back and forth that ultimately contributes to a richer conversation. What's more, they then learn the art of questioning, too, and they get stronger at eliciting our ideas back. They first need to be heard. It is with this backdrop of authentic oral storytelling and natural listening, questioning, and conversing with caregivers that we turn toward building bridges with more robust and thoughtful talk in the classroom, too.

## Connecting

The love of listening to and telling stories—an oral tradition as deep as history itself—is one we, as educators, try to instill in our classroom every day. "The stories we tell about ourselves help us understand who we are, how our lives developed, and how they could have unfolded differently. But we also find meaning in stories told by others. Whether in fiction or film, on the radio or on the stage, stories about others can help us reflect on our own values and experiences," writes Emily Esfahani Smith, in *The Power of Meaning: Crafting a Life That Matters* (2017). It's why we choose joyful read-alouds to share as a classroom community, and it's the reason we hold group conversations to share the work that made us proud. Zaretta Hammond, in *Culturally Responsive Teaching and the Brain*, echoes that stories prime young brains for learning because stories build rapport and make us feel safe (2014), saying, "Neuroscience tells us the brain feels safest and relaxed when we are connected to others we trust to treat us well." Put another way, with strong storytelling that lulls, connects, intrigues, and inspires, our fight-or-flight responses are subdued, and empathy for one another increases.

## Instruction That Elevates Oral Storytelling and Community Questioning

Recall our earlier conversation about interviewing and sharing the stories of family members and loved ones. Caregivers can orchestrate similar moves, too, echoing these powerful conversations in the home. Educators Luz Herrera and Carla España write about the importance of learning more about our own stories from families and friends by including lessons around oral history in *En Comunidad: Lessons for Centering the Voices and Experiences of Bilingual Latinx Students*. Learning the wisdom and stories of our elders grows identity-rich conversations and understanding. They suggest asking questions like *What places are special to you?* and *Have you ever had a challenging time communicating with others?* (2020). Building on the research of critical race scholar Pedro Nava, they write: "We believe in the strength, wisdom and healing across community knowledge, abuelita knowledge, and other funds of knowledge that are often dismissed in schools. Acknowledging these ways of knowing and bringing them into our curriculum validates what students have learned from their families and creates spaces for students' bilingualism and their Latinx identities." This is important literacy work, but it also anchors kids in curiosity, questions, and conversations.

Oral storytelling exists in every single culture and in every single home—caregivers incorporate it naturally. And oral storytelling, as its own communication genre, can be a rigorous form of composition and learning when woven into classroom design. We can teach students to brainstorm narrative ideas by asking them whose stories they'd like to learn more about and exalt them by sharing. The flowchart in Figure 5.1 (page 126) represents a general structure for crafting units around oral storytelling.

**FIGURE 5.1**
*This flowchart shows a simple path for students to take
their own oral storytelling ideas through a composition process.*

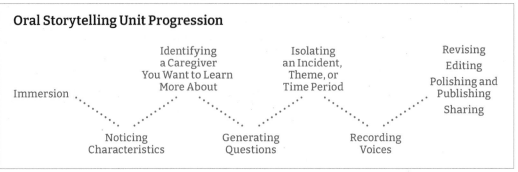

The first part of any oral storytelling project includes immersion in the genre. I suggest that teachers share clips from StoryCorps (storycorps.org) and lead an inquiry with students to list the characteristics of the genre. Students typically notice that example stories include multiple voices and emotion in the verbal intonation and that the clips are focused on a specific incident, theme, or time period. Then, we move into brainstorming who they might interview and what they might ask. You'll want to be sensitive to the ways you frame and assign family interviews so as not to alienate or exclude students with different family makeups. I suggest using inclusive language like *your grownups, community*, and *chosen family* and add caveats that stories from anyone in a child's collective are valuable. Oftentimes, students will be excited to learn more about their grandparents or an aunt or uncle, and talking with peers allows them to generate additional ideas for folks in their collective from whom they want to learn. For example, one student in a Southside Chicago classroom shared that he loves his neighbor because they always play checkers together after school. When he realized he could generate questions to learn more about his neighbor's life, like where he grew up and what his favorite songs were as a child, a powerful interview sequence was unlocked. The student realized his neighbor likely had lots of stories to share. What kinds of questions might students ask to get their family and loved ones to open up?

◈ Tell me about an emotional moment that never leaves you.

◈ What is one memory you hope to carry with you forever?

◈ Can you describe a moment you had as a young person that taught you a lesson in hindsight about life?

◈ Do you have any regrets? Why or why not?

◈ What are you especially proud of accomplishing in your life?

◈ Describe the place where you grew up.

◈ What was one formative experience that you believe shaped you?

◈ What decision in your life was especially hard to make?

◈ Can you describe a time that was particularly challenging for you? How did you process your way through it?

◈ Who is in your support circle? Who is in the village that raised you? What do you especially appreciate about these people in your life?

◈ What advice do you have for me that you now know because you've lived longer than I have?

◈ What is particularly different now in the world (or in our city, town, neighborhood) from when you were growing up? What is similar?

Once students have a sense of who they want to interview for their project and what they're aiming to ask, we prep for the interview portion by reading excerpts from Sherry Turkle's *Reclaiming Conversation: The Power of Talk in a Digital Age* (2016), which explains the importance of fluid conversation building and eye contact when possible in conversation with individuals, should the students be in the same physical space as their interview subjects. Continuing in the composition process, students listen back to their interviews to select which clips are most striking. It is powerful when they invite peers to listen to their recordings alongside them and help decide which parts are most interesting and important.

Last, we lead workshops to help students revise and edit their chosen clips, polishing their work by adding their own transitions, introductions, or conclusions to the oral recordings. We think too about how we will share these recordings with a wider audience, either through social media, online in a blog space, or posted on devices around the room for direct listening. Our students are always growing as writers, and practice in oral communication supports this. We cannot seek excellence with the pen or the word processor if we have not heard it with our ears and felt it in our hearts. Projects like this help kids to do exactly that.

*Middle school students in Chicago's Albany Park neighborhood engage in oral conversation.*

## The Power of Talk in Our Education Spaces

We don't often validate talk alone as a critically important piece of literacy learning, yet when we ask students to compose, we almost always ask them to orally rehearse first. Or perhaps we don't consider talk, storytelling, and discussion as components to grow and assess, because they're not visible the way tangible, written composition and assignments are. But as literacy teachers, when we transition students from idea building to recording those ideas on paper, don't we usually start with getting them to verbalize an idea conjured in their mind? This first step of the writing process—talking about ideas aloud—is a clear entry point for caregivers of all cultures and abilities to engage.

Often, young kids have more sophisticated oral language than they do mastery of letters and sounds. As a result, we often ask students in PreK–2 to first say aloud what they mean to write. They can record themselves using a variety of tech options (e.g., Mote or Google Voice Recorder), or they can simply share aloud with a partner before moving to the page, drawing, labeling, and stretching out sounds. For students to see tangible evidence of their conversations, I like to use blocks or Legos at the center of tables or in partnerships and ask students to build a discussion tower. As each child contributes to the conversation, they can add a block. This simple exercise has encouraged previously reserved students to contribute more readily to their peers' thoughts, especially when paired with scaffolded sentence frames like *I also think*, or *Have you considered . . . ?* I often cut discussion stems into strips and leave them in cups on student tables for them to pull from and use until their natural instinct for conversations kicks in.

Audio recording has also proven to be an effective revision tool in the drafting process for students, particularly for multilingual students, because they can read their piece aloud and hear where they had intended it to sound differently. Not only does this practice communicate to students that the writing process can look all sorts of ways, but it also gives them the opportunity to translanguage, inserting different languages where it feels natural. And audio recordings of published compositions feel like a gift to readers and listeners, too.

Educator and author of *Building Bigger Ideas: A Process for Teaching Purposeful Talk*, Maria Nichols suggests three practices we can use when building purposeful talk. First, we can "gently focus" children on the preferred talk behaviors, like eye contact, nodding along, and adding on. Second, we can "authentically facilitate" by observing how children are engaging with each other's ideas and helping them volley the conversation back and forth, and third, we can offer clear feedback on what we notice about how the talk is flowing. Nichols suggests modeling flexibility while avoiding "right answerism," so that children experience sitting in the discomfort of no right or wrong answers (2019). Caregivers, too, can replicate these coaching techniques if we share these processes with them.

## Instruction That Gives Voice to Process

Every morning when our daughter Ezzy wakes up, she beelines to a framed image of a bunny getting ready for the day. It's a colorful illustration we picked up on a road trip to Montreal, and, though she can't read the French captions, the series of images offers a blueprint for her morning routine.

Still rubbing her eyes, she says aloud, sticking a finger up with each step: "First, brush my teeth. Next, wash my face. Then, pick my clothes. Okay," she nods. "After that, do my hair, then eat breakfast." Having given voice to her morning routine, she plods down the hall, ready to start her day.

We connect to this valuable idea in our classrooms all the time. In reading instruction, we ask young students to tell across their fingers what happened *first*, *next*, and *then* when recounting a story's plot. We teach kids to share one by one the facts they learned in a nonfiction text, putting up a finger with each fact they name. In writing instruction, we teach students to use their fingers as a natural graphic organizer to plan their writing: naming steps of a how-to or teaching book, listing ideas for an argument essay, or saying aloud details to back up their opinions. We teach students to rehearse their stories aloud for a partner, telling each part piece by piece, so they can change the story if it doesn't flow fluidly. We coach students to say across their hand what they did *first*, *next*, and *after* for a personal narrative, putting up a finger for each scene to write across multiple pages. At the end of lessons and gatherings, teachers might ask students to name across their fingers their plan for independent work time, including what materials they need to gather and how they'll approach their reading or writing work for the day.

In our classrooms, we teach children to turn their thoughts into words and words into writing. We know, as educators, that oral rehearsal as a way of prewriting is useful before putting pencil to paper (or finger to keyboard). In fact, educators who broaden what has traditionally been seen as written composition (Coppola 2019) are asking children to develop multimodal writing that includes podcast creation and annotated soundtracks, expanded ways of composing built on organized oral language. We teach children that there is no idea in their mind that they cannot give words to so it can be manifested on the page.

Whether we're encouraging storytelling units, inviting students to talk through ideas, or showing children how to articulate parts of their learning process, we'll want to make sure that parents understand the why behind these practices.

Figure 5.2 showcases additional instructional interactions grounded in talk that we might need to clarify. What would you and your colleagues add to these considerations to communicate connections between school and home more clearly?

# More Ways to Explore the Power of Talk

Sharing learning experiences together while exploring a variety of resources will always be one of the best ways families can support the power of talk. Here are a few favorites to keep the conversation going with kids, caretakers, and educators.

| Text Title | Author |
|---|---|
| *I'm From* (2023) | Gary Gray Jr.<br>Illustrated by Oge Mora |
| *The Night Before Freedom:<br>A Juneteenth Story* (2023) | Glenda Armand<br>Illustrated by Corey Barksdale |
| *The Artivist* (2023) | Nikkolas Smith |
| *The Shape of Thunder* (2021) | Jasmine Warga |
| *Wild Tongues Can't Be Tamed:<br>15 Voices from the Latinx Diaspora* (2021) | Edited by Saraceia J. Fennell |
| *Only This Beautiful Moment* (2023) | Abdi Nazemian |

**FIGURE 5.2**
*Talk-Focused Instruction to Clarify with Caregivers*

| Literacy<br>Classroom Practice | What Might Not Be Clear to Caregivers |
|---|---|
| Frequent use of turn and talk | Caregivers may not see the immediate value in increased talk, but the more kids talk, the more they learn. In class, partner and group talk routines create the space for MORE talk. If kids talk only to the teachers, each student will never get the amount of time on tasks necessary for practice and growth. By using partners and groups, the quantity of talk goes up. Caregivers may not know that encouraging this beyond school by asking kids to comment on everything will support our work, too. Discussing meals, songs, shows, games, images on screens, advertisements, random occurrences, and news is the kind of abundant talk at home that fuels measurable literacy growth at school. |

FIGURE 5.2 *(continued)*

| Literacy Classroom Practice | What Might Not Be Clear to Caregivers |
|---|---|
| Conferring in a workshop setting | Make sure to continue clarifying for caregivers that when learning is personalized, children go further. Allowing caregivers to see that we individualize learning by spending time with each learner builds the kind of trust between caregivers and teachers that leads to stronger bonds. Beyond this, conferring with students is a powerful way to learn a student's individual strengths OUTSIDE of traditional forms of testing or assessment. We can communicate to caregivers that this kind of one-on-one conversational teaching allows teachers to accelerate and track student growth in areas of concern. |
| Socratic seminar | Though caregivers might intuitively know that Socratic seminars are an opportunity for kids to show their thinking, we will want to communicate that like any other "project," these experiences require preparation. However, they allow teachers to see how learners think flexibly and in response to new ideas presented by their peers. Caregivers can also connect to this at home by discussing ideas with kids. They can extend those ideas by asking questions like *Why?* or *What makes you think this?* We can clarify for caregivers that these conversations are often tricky, but they help kids think with complexity—something we want them doing for the rest of their lives. |
| Talking through plans for writing, goal setting, research activities, and project development | Nothing can happen without a plan, and teaching children to visualize a goal and plan toward it is one of the most important life skills to practice. We can clarify for caregivers that encouraging kids to plan how a meal can go, what they will do during a trip to the bathroom, what happens for bedtime routines, or what we might talk about when we phone relatives helps young people set priorities, identify steps, and see process. Caregivers will want to know that this planning is important for literacy, just as it's important for life. |
| Morning messages and meetings, along with soft starts | Caregivers will appreciate knowing that morning messages and meetings help young people to set goals and intentions for the day. It allows them to process life outside of school and to think about how they want to be in school. Although caregivers might not think this is actual instruction, we'll want to share that these gatherings are effective transitions from one part of the day into another. Talk-rich moments like this position children to do their best, and caregivers will value trying these same moves at home. |

*(continued)*

FIGURE 5.2 *(continued)*

| Literacy Classroom Practice | What Might Not Be Clear to Caregivers |
|---|---|
| Student-led family conferences for grade and growth sharing | Caregivers might not realize that student-led family conferences are an opportunity for young people to reflect and to share that reflection with the people who matter to them. When kids lead conferences, it demonstrates sharing of power—that the adults are not the only ones who get to talk or think about how school is going. Caregivers are often conditioned to listen for what other adults think. Kids also think lots about their experience at school. Caregivers will want to hear directly from teachers that learning to listen to children is a valuable lesson for the entire community. We can share with caregivers that practicing reflection at home can impact how kids learn, lead, and deal with difficulty. |

## Elevating

I will never forget my parents descending on my apartment after the birth of my first daughter and the image of my father cradling baby Eliana in the crook of his arm while he quietly described in Farsi the trees and sunshine outside the window.

"You aren't talking enough to her," my father chided me. "Tell her stories."

I was raw with emotion and annoyed by these comments at the time. It wasn't until later that I recognized this particular advice as more than just an outdated parenting hack. Without even consciously trying, caregivers, no matter their language, can authentically build the foundation of literacy.

But how can we encourage caregivers to continue these valuable conversations as their children grow beyond their earliest years? How can we continue to emphasize the importance of storytelling and narration of ordinary activities amid the flurry of worksheets, assignments, and evaluations that are sent home to keep caregivers apprised of their children's progress?

We can make suggestions grounded in the premise that all talk, all stories, all conversations contribute to literary progress. Make up stories about characters from cereal boxes. Build on each other's stories by starting a sentence when you walk, asking each kid in the family to add on. Set up toys, pretending they talk to each other as you creatively build background for their characters. Who are they? What traits do they have? What is their relationship? What is the conflict in the story and the connection between incidents? These are the building blocks of narrative writing and traditional fiction story arc; this practice builds brainstorming skills we'll also practice in the classroom.

## Extending Talk at Home

Of all the family engagement strategies in this book, emphasizing with caregivers the value of talk in the home—any kind of talk—is perhaps the most straightforward. It is also perhaps the most effective. We hold this at the core of our holistic literacy instruction, and we want caregivers to know it, too. No matter what is happening around you: talk.

When caring for our youngest children, filling the empty space with stories and descriptive talk is almost instinctual. Singing songs and nursery rhymes, flipping slowly through picture books, and naming letters and sounds comes naturally; after all, that's often how we learned ourselves. Perhaps it is no surprise, then, that these techniques almost universally elicit coos of excitement and happiness from these little learners. But it's important to continue conversation with our middle grade students, too. I think about teenagers who are more prone to isolating themselves; about my own daughter Eliana, who would choose to video call Chicago friends before engaging in conversation with us; who needs goading and listening to and support navigating tricky conversations more than my youngest kids. As educators, we might share ideas with caregivers for building talk and conversation with kids of all ages, such as:

◈ **Languages.** Remind families to speak in any and all languages they have in their repertoires. All languages are an important and critical part of children's robust literacy learning and can be peppered in or spoken solely at any time of day, both inside and outside of the school building. Marie Garza, principal of Albany Park Multicultural Academy in Chicago's diverse North Side neighborhood, said, "Our families see their inability to speak English as a deficit even when we don't say that. They see it as a barrier, when I want to message the opposite." Personally, I know there were times when my own family felt embarrassed to speak Farsi or Arabic; when they would want to speak English to show they could. No language is meant to be checked upon entry like luggage when children enter the literacy classroom. We need to actively elevate for families that all languages are valid, worthy, and important, encouraging them to switch between languages where and when it feels natural, and reminding them what an asset it is to know more than one language.

## WE DON'T NEED TO TALK THE SAME

Linguistic justice really stems from the foundational belief that, just as there's no one way to be human, there's no one way to express being human. The geography, politics, and circumstances of our world have pushed people into different patterns and forms of expression. All of these forms reflect the power, beauty, and genius of the communities from which they emerged. These unique expressive forms often merge with other linguistic patterns, meeting at the crossroads of art and digital media and proliferating through youth Internet culture, fashion, and music. Despite the syntactical and communicative genius evident in these emergent forms of communication, specific forms of expression—such as those of white men—have been deemed more professional, artful, and functional than others. Linguistic justice demands that we reject the idea that genius can be expressed only in what's considered standard English (Flores and Rosa 2015; Baker-Bell 2020). People all over the world have internalized the falsehood that to sound this way is what it means to be smart. Accents, nonstandard forms of the language, using invented vocabulary—all have been considered "less acceptable" in certain circles. To learn more, read the scholarship of Ofelia Garcia on translanguaging; Nelson Flores and Jonathan Rosa on "undoing appropriateness" in raciolinguistic ideologies and language diversity in education; April Baker-Bell's *Linguistic Justice: Black Language, Literacy, Identity and Pedagogy* (2020); and Angel Jones's *Street Scholar* (2022).

◈ **Word Swap:** Encourage caregivers to be honest with their children about their own language abilities and swap out naturally when they need to substitute in a different language. I watched my mother do this without thinking when she was reading a book to my daughter about animals, translating the English book to Farsi as she was reading, and stopped at the word *squirrel*. My mother couldn't call up the Farsi translation and told Eloisa that she was just going to switch to English. These sorts of natural language maneuvers are critically important for students to witness and see modeled, so that they feel empowered to do the same. Kaveh Akbar, an Iranian American poet and scholar, speaks about the "delta" between languages, where there's space for interpretation and elevation of discourse when you realize, as a person playing with words, that different languages exist and that different words connote different meanings (Akbar 2022) When we make languages and word swaps transparent for students to understand, revealing there's no right or wrong, but rather different nuances and connotations connected to different words, we are making space for elevated critical thinking.

◈ **Synonym Games.** Caregivers can make language and word games fun by trying different synonyms for mundane words like *small* or *large* and *mad* or *sad*. In the classroom, we often shade synonyms on word gradient charts, connecting shades of colors with meaning of words. Linking colors to word meaning helps words become more sticky and contextualized for children.

◈ **Suggest Book Titles That Celebrate Words.** Share with caregivers titles of texts to read aloud at home that include characters who talk and play with words for fun. Some of these might include *Stacey's Extraordinary Words* (2021), *The Word Collector* (2018), and *Digging for Words: José Alberto Gutiérrez and the Library He Built* (2020). I like to pair these with *Ralph Tells a Story* (2012) to talk about the power of words in telling stories and reading with joy, love, and authenticity.

◈ **Let Your Tween Talk.** As my children grow older, at times I find it harder to relate to them. Ehsan talks about Dungeons and Dragons and March Madness, whereas Eliana talks about wispy bangs and the music from *In the Heights.* If I'm being honest, I had a disconnect with my own parents when I was the same age, perhaps because my parents were not interested in American pop culture. I have to check myself and appreciate the topics my kids *are* excited about and naturally want to tell me. Recognizing that our young people are learning a ton in the navigation of these social literacies as tweens and listening with open ears and hearts will make way for more conversation with our kids, regardless of their age. As educators, we might simply share a few talk and listening stems so caregivers can give their middle-grade students space. Question starters like *What made you laugh today?* or even *When did you feel awesome today?* usually prime my older kids for talking. Let them lead.

## Read What You're Reading, Aloud

One move I love to share with others that is wildly successful for me and some of my friends is to read aloud to our kids whatever adult book we are already reading. At first I thought it was background noise, but then my children began asking questions about the plot and characters or information in my books,

*Grownups reading their own books aloud grows literacy.*

picking up on bits and pieces that surprised me. That simple act worked twofold, both showing them that their mother is a reader and also growing their listening brains. My childhood friend's father was in graduate school when she was a baby, and he used to read medical texts aloud to her; I always joked that her vocabulary was enormous on account of her very big brain. Little did I know that decades ago, Dr. Schmidhofer was naturally practicing my exact parenting move.

## Giving Voice to Processes in the Home

Recall our earlier discussion about how we give voice to processes in our reading and writing instruction. We suggest that caregivers do the same by giving voice to process at home as a bridge to classroom work, so students have experience naming steps and explaining aloud the order for tasks they do. It might mean reminding caregivers to make their thinking transparent for kids around them, giving voice to the tasks they do naturally around the home.

Also effective is giving voice to process around emotions and frustrations, listing aloud steps for how one might 1. pause, 2. rewind, and 3. calm down, or how one might 1. stop, 2. take a deep breath, and 3. try again. With four young children running around, there isn't a week (day? afternoon?) where I don't feel my emotions bubble to the surface because I'm human. Showing my imperfections by naming my emotions aloud for my kids has always seemed to help them process, too.

Here are some additional—sometimes silly—ideas to share with caregivers that will feel inviting without being challenging or burdensome:

◈ **Retell** when you get home what you did at the park, zoo, or doctor's office. For our youngest family members, it's helpful to stick up a finger each time you make a move. *First, we waited for the bus. Next, we got off after eleven stops. Then, we walked two blocks. It was chilly!*

◈ **Explain** your process for managing emotions or calming down in simple sentences across your hand. For example, a caregiver might say *Ugh, I asked twice for you to run outside instead of around the dining room table where I am taking a Zoom call. I'm going to take a WOW moment: 1. wait (puts a finger up), 2. oxygen (takes a deep breath), 3. water (hydrates). Did you see how I just cooled down by taking a WOW moment?*

◈ **Generate a list** together orally for getting ready for a specific event or day, perhaps leading with a question. *What do we need to do to prepare for Teta's visit? Hmm. We need to wash the sheets and organize where she'll sleep (one finger up). What else? We need to buy her favorite (chamomile!) tea (another finger up).*

◈ **Name** aloud step by step what caregivers are doing to prepare something, however simple or intricate. Lean into whatever you already do, from the niche hobby to the mundane. If they're into taking photos, explain to kids what they're doing when they change their lens. If they're putting the dishes away, explain their process for that, too. It doesn't need to be glamorous.

◈ **Ask** that kids give adults (or older siblings to younger) instructions on how to make or do something, which especially makes them feel empowered. *I love that haunted house you drew! Can you show me? Can you name the steps aloud?*

◈ **Notice** and name when something goes wrong, and talk through problem-solving together, revising instructions as you go. Kids can problem-solve mishaps like getting ready for a trip without packing toothbrushes, preparing for a doctor's appointment but forgetting the time, getting on the train going the wrong way, changing clothes to go for a run only to realize it's pouring, or getting ready to watch a sporting event at a friend's but omitting an essential ingredient to the dish they were slated to bring.

◈ **Talk** out directions to go to a friend's house instead of relying on GPS.

◈ **Find** other authentic reasons to talk through lists, like instructions for taking care of a pet or a plant when you're away from home.

*Caregivers and their children in Jersey City, giving voice to process: writing letters in the mud, noting observations while swinging, chatting while playing soccer.*

No matter what style they use, caregivers can naturally work conversations into children's home lives, especially when they see how doing so promotes learning at school as well. These types of conversations might seem simple, but it is the very same way we coach kids to think when planning their writing, retelling parts of a book, or problem-solving when an attempt goes wrong or a strategy isn't quite as helpful as they'd originally thought. Conversations like these get kids acclimated to naming what they *already do, need to do, or know how to do*, which empowers them to feel more confident when talking about their ideas in the classroom. Let's help parents make that connection, too.

# Elevating Caregiver Involvement Around Talk

| If you're focusing on . . . at school . . . | Caregivers might . . . |
|---|---|
| Turn and talk during direct instruction | Focus efforts at home on being attentive to one-on-one conversations between family members, paying close attention to how they lean in, talk with their hands, add to the conversation, and ask questions. |
| Peer conversations about independent reading books | Ask questions about student independent reading, leaning into natural curiosities about why the child enjoys the text, what the child is learning, what stories it reminds them of, and what connections they can make. Caregivers might want to share about their own reading with children. |
| Debates and argument composition | Encourage their children to back up their opinions at home with facts to better prove their points. They might prompt their kids to organize their thinking with big ideas and reasons their argument holds and even think of potential counterarguments, so they can argue with more passion. |
| Soft starts and invitations for learning based on visuals, reading, or other activities that include student talk | Mirror this in-school process with gentle prompts for conversation that don't always communicate necessity, direction, or learning but instead connect more readily to their children personally. Educator and activist Sara K. Ahmed, author of *Being the Change: Lessons and Strategies to Teach Social Comprehension*, says "The learning begins with how you entered the space, not the sound of my voice" (2023). |

## Inviting

As a child, I woke to the sound of my parents' voices. They talked incessantly. Their together time was before the sun rose, and I would listen to them debating elaborate plans in the darkness, until I would clamber downstairs, marking a new day but not the end of their storytelling.

When evening fell, I would perch on the kitchen counter and listen to my aunts chatter while making rice. My favorite stories were about their childhood in Iran: sleeping on the roof to escape the summer heat, biking to buy chocolate milk, crafting their own kites. I fell in love with their words.

Talking about the past, honoring stories of where we came from, explaining the meaning behind our names, talking about how best friends met, how our chosen family came to laugh and grieve together, and reminiscing about people in our community are all integral parts of literacy growth. These conversations can be part of the ongoing quest to know who we are, where we come from, and what we stand for. This is holistic literacy practice.

## Considerations for Inviting Caregivers to Elevate the Power of the Collective with Their Children

As teachers, the more we share of ourselves by bringing our own stories alive, the more apt our children are to share about themselves in their writing, connections to reading, and community conversations. In a similar way, when we ask students to close their eyes and picture the mental movies of their stories on their "brain TVs," we are emulating the ways we put our personal stories on paper. Caregivers can join in this process by sharing family stories at home as they often do, and, as teachers, we can remind them that this *is literacy teaching*.

## Community Stories

We can arm caregivers with countless suggestions for making these conversations more robust to help bridge our work between the home and school, enhancing what families already do to fortify their self-identity and rich histories. Other home activities we might suggest to continue strengthening our levels of collective care include:

◈ Sit down with family and community **photos** from the past to tell stories about when, where, and why the images were taken. Allow kids to ask questions and look at all parts of the photos. Photos can open the pathway to so much questioning, conversation, and connection. For example, in the image here of me with my father and uncle circa 1988, I might ask

*Where were we going? Was my hair often in pigtails? Why were we dressed up? What city were we in? Who took the photo? Why were we together? Who put me on the car? How long after you emigrated from Iran was this? Had you finished college? Was Uncle Jalal already married?*

*Nawal with her father and uncle, 1988.*

❖ **Call** a relative or family friend to ask questions like *How old were you when . . . ? Tell me about a time when you . . . ? What's one of your favorite memories from when . . . ? Do you remember when I . . . ?*

❖ Put together a **timeline** of photographs from the child's life to revisit and reminisce. Print cell phone photos at a local pharmacy kiosk and string them up. Conversations might begin with one photograph, and before long, caregivers are exchanging additional stories promoted from memories beyond physical images.

❖ Review **newspapers or magazines** together, and let children ask questions. *What do you see that's interesting or shocking? What are you wondering about? What questions do you have?* Suggest that caregivers model this practice by naming what's interesting, curious, or strange to them, too.

Although these types of discussions support the conversations children have in their classrooms every day, they're also critical for maintaining their connection to their past and shaping the adult humans they'll eventually become. I love the words of Yaa Gyasi, who writes in *Transcendent Kingdom*: "There's a picture of my family . . . I think I remember that day, but I don't know if I've just turned my mother's stories about it into memories or if I've stared at that picture long enough that my own stories started to emerge" (2020). There's a similar vein of nostalgia that runs deep in my family. Simple anecdotes from the pasts of our friends and family encourage speaking, listening, and knowing one another, and this storytelling cultivates literacy skills.

## Narrate Your World and Question Everything

My husband and I chuckle every time we drive anywhere with my mother-in-law because she reads aloud every single sign she sees, regardless of language. She'll read "Tax Attorney," "*Muebleria*," and "Zoo," as if we can't also see the signs, and we often wonder why she feels compelled to voice these mundane discoveries with the wonder of a safari guide.

The truth is she's probably in the habit of doing this from her days as a school teacher and principal in New Jersey. This form of narrating the world around us and naming what we see is beneficial for kids of all ages but particularly for the very young. It is critical that we message to caregivers that any talk is supportive talk, particularly when it's explanatory and detailed. When we care for babies and toddlers, we might point to everything out of the window like my mother-in-law does, saying aloud, *See the bus? The bus is long! There are two sets of doors! In the front AND the back. Some people are sitting in seats, and others are standing. Oh, I see bicycles being carried on the front, too.* Hearing all kinds of language and words makes a massive difference in a child's literacy development, especially in the early years. Children won't remember every word that they hear, but they begin to build patterns of speech and syntax. They learn what the people around them talk about, care about, and value. This is not just linguistic growth; it is cultural growth. This kind of talk contributes so much to who kids are and who they will become.

Younger kids tend to ask questions about their surroundings. But we want to encourage older kids to question the world around them, too, applying a critical lens to all that they absorb. Caregivers might lean into this by narrating their inner thinking and questioning. Rather than just pointing out a billboard while driving down the highway, they might ask *How long do you think that billboard has been up there? Who owns that billboard? Do you think that's a good advertising strategy?* After watching a movie, they might ask their teenagers, *What do you think were all the roles that went into making that movie? How long do you think it took to produce it? Which parts did you like or wish they omitted?* It's not important that caregivers know the answers to these questions. The point is to engage the teenagers to take the conversation from beyond simple observations to more of a discussion that makes way for more talk, moving seamlessly between drawing conclusions to building stories about what they're seeing, so when they write themselves or describe their reading, they're more able to build a narrative behind their thoughts, too. Questions to get these conversations started and keep them going might include:

◈ How do you think that was made?

◈ Who do you think paid for it? How was it funded?

◈ Who is left out of the story? Whose perspective do you think was missing?

◈ What do you think was there before? What do you think came first?

◈ What do you think might happen next?

◈ Who owns or controls it?

◈ Who benefits from this change?

◈ What variations or versions could we imagine that might work better?

◈ How might we design this more equitably?

Although oral storytelling and building talk is a natural part of the caregiving experience, we can be thoughtful about how to elevate natural language practices of families into our classroom experiences, and how we can share with families easy-to-implement ideas that will continue to amplify those at-home conversations. If our goal is to establish nourishing caregiver collaborations while cultivating rich readers, writers, and thinkers whose discussion and oral stories are creative and constant, we can use families' authentic conversational tendencies to our advantage in education spaces, too.

## Reflecting: Talk: The Power of Oral Conversation to Grow Ideas and Connect Us

| | |
|---|---|
| In what specific ways are your students already talking with families and caregivers at home and in their communities that support the power of expanding relationships through conversations, talking through processes, and storytelling? | Think about a student who is especially quiet in class. Have you observed this child being more vocal in other school spaces? In other classrooms? How might you make the child feel more comfortable building talk in your space? |
| | |
| How might you engage families and caregivers to continue building talk with their children? | What shared literacy experiences can you cultivate for students and their families that might lead to more talk? |
| | |
| What questioning stems seem especially pertinent for your students' families and could be readily translated to a variety of contexts, including alphabetic text, the environment, images, or media? | How might you make conversations more visible as an artifact of learning in your classroom community? |
| | |

# Reflection Space

Feel free to use this additional space to process the reflection questions and your own thinking from this chapter.

# Chapter 6
# Choice: Freeing Students to Make Self-Driven Decisions

When Eliana was eleven, the two of us went to the mall together to find her an outfit for her sixth-grade science fair, where she was going to present on Newton's laws and show off her miniature Rube Goldberg machine. The music was blasting; we knew the words to half the songs. It felt like the first alone time I'd had with her in so long, given our recent family move. We were both laughing and in genuinely good moods. Each outfit seemed more hilarious than the last, as we hastily tore clothes off and on, wanting to hit as many stores as we could in the rare window of time we had.

"Mom," Eliana said. "Those sleeves look ridiculous. Move on."

We were having a blast. Then Eliana put on a little shirt with pretty puffy sleeves but no fabric covering her stomach at all. The pattern was beautiful, reminding me of our gorgeous kilims. The colors were muted but rich; it was youthful. Eliana grinned.

"I love this," she said, sort of spinning before the mirror. "Do you?"

Something flared inside me. My first instinct was to say absolutely not. My parents would never have let me out of the house wearing that when I was her age. Was it appropriate? She seemed so happy. I took a beat. For whom was I policing her freedom of expression? Was I just wielding power because I said so, with no real reason? Perhaps I'd be embarrassed in front of the other parents. Or maybe she'd seem less studious or serious about her presentation. This suddenly made no sense to me. How could her clothing affect the quality of her work? I was imposing an outdated belief system on my daughter without much more to say than "because I said so."

We left with the shirt.

So much of what we have come to accept about teaching is about policing children. We tell them where to be and when; how long to sit and in what position; what to touch or not touch; what to say, write, do. We do things in ways that have always been done because we're scared to push back, make change, and sit in the discomfort of it. Even though it might challenge us when students make choices we wouldn't personally, like Eliana did with her shirt, does it really matter?

The pedagogy in this chapter is centered on choice. It is one of the hardest things in all of teaching to embrace. What's the balance between telling children what to do and allowing them to choose what works best for them? The choices we give children allow them the agency to take their own paths, make their own mistakes, and determine what's best for themselves. When we share decision-making power with children, we free them from the limits of our own thinking. Despite our best efforts, there is so much about their lives that we do not see. At times, we may draw conclusions that are not always right, equitable, or reasonable. Not only are children more excited to learn when they have the power to make decisions about their journeys, they're more likely to trust us. It shows we believe in them. It gives them space to make mistakes and to learn from them. Ultimately, it gives them space to become who they want to be. This is the greatest gift that education can proffer.

## Listening

One day I was with my kids in Hamilton Park, near Jersey City, when my son, Ehsan, asked if we could pick up his library holds. Ezzy, his little sister, refused to leave the park. This happens often in a family of our size, with four kids who have competing interests and desires for how time should be spent. It takes a significant amount of negotiating to maneuver the whole family away from an activity and into another one without planting the seed first.

"I don't want to go," Ezzy said. "I want to swing."

"Stay swinging!" Eloisa chimed in agreement.

Ezzy is the third of my children. She likes to know what to expect and how the flow of a day will go and doesn't like when things are out of place. Though she shares a room with her little sister, she hides many of her treasured belongings under her bed, lined up and hidden by a neat row of stuffies. Nobody is to touch her special things. Recently, she asked if she could take violin lessons. When I asked why the violin, instead of piano like her sister, she admitted she didn't want to play an instrument she would have to share. I understand this.

"Do you want to go to the library now or later?" I asked her.

Ezzy thought for a moment, pumped her legs, and then said, "Later."

"When you go to the library, do you want to check out books or color the pages the librarian prints out?" I asked next.

She seemed to ignore me but a beat later, she asked, "Are there books about clouds at the library?"

I smiled. I looked up at the sky. It had grown ominously dark. I remembered how both Eliana and Ehsan loved the sound of repeating "cumulonimbus" after me, when I had borrowed Gail Gibbons's book, *Weather Words and What They Mean* (1990) and how we had painted fluffy clouds after observing them in the Chicago skies when we lived there.

"Yes, baby, are you interested in learning about clouds?" I helped her off the swing, with one eye on Eloisa, who was toddling around beside us.

Ezzy paused for a moment then responded, "No, actually, I want to learn more about ice cream."

## Honoring

So much of parenting includes offering choice to our children, dozens of times a day, perhaps without even realizing it. This isn't necessarily a parenting move that is taught, but it is one I have seen over and over in every sort of household as a way to handle obstinate children; as a way to give kids agency over what they do, wear, or eat; as a way to involve children in the direction of their own lives, however small those choices might seem.

For example, a series of errands on a Saturday afternoon might require lots of waiting, which, for a kid, can be difficult. They can feel powerless during an afternoon of buzzing from place to place with their parents at the whim of stock clerks, cashiers, bank tellers, and hair stylists. We might offer them a choice as a break from the necessary fatigue of these moments. "We are going to the pharmacy for two things: sunscreen and bug spray. Which one should we pick up first?" On the surface this choice means very little. But the act of making this choice suggests to a young person that their insight matters. Wielding even this small power sends the message that your youth does not mean that you don't matter, and it allows kids to practice the kind of adaptive decision making that leaders employ daily. We cannot say that kids are "the leaders of tomorrow" with one breath while denying them opportunities to lead with the next.

This inclusive stance has real implications for the classroom, too—from independent reading to options for flexible seating to partnerships for classwork; from choice in how to represent thinking to choice in what shows up on classroom walls and when those visuals get swapped out. When students have the chance to make decisions over what they learn and how they learn, they're not only more willing and enthusiastic to participate in their learning processes, but their learning becomes more genuine, sticky, and authentic (Minor 2019).

## Connecting

Our children are born curious. They are naturally interested in the world around them and inclined to piece together the way their environments are built to understand their place in it. In the classroom, we know that when we let students lead with their natural curiosities, they are more engaged. No adult wants to study and research something they feel no interest in; neither do our children. We see time and time again that when students choose their writing topics and hand-pick their independent reading books; when they decide what they want to research or how they want to share artifacts of their learning, they more easily grow. In *Reading for Their Life: (Re)Building the Textual Lineage of African American Adolescent Males*, Alfred Tatum discusses following kids' interests. The things that thrill, perplex, or fascinate them in the world are the same things that will keep them engaged in the classroom. We know, too, that many of our schools tend to unintentionally stifle student imaginations across time and that as students move forward in their academic careers, they see creativity as less valuable to the way school works (Tatum 2009). Though they don't all say this with words, most caregivers want their students to springboard learning from natural curiosity. Some might be thinking about increased use of AI technology and ChatGPT, acknowledging that in an age where computers generate full-length research papers within minutes, ingenuity and compassion will become their children's greatest assets.

> **Our children are born curious. They are naturally interested in the world around them and inclined to piece together the way their environments are built to understand their place in it. In the classroom, we know that when we let students lead with their natural curiosities, they are more engaged.**

Others might be thinking about the dynamic needs of a twenty-first-century workforce where so much of leadership comes down to creative problem-solving. In a gig economy, even your Uber driver is their own CEO. Problem-solving is in everyone's job description.

What's more, students with robust and nuanced social literacies in outside-of-school activities like Minecraft or Beyblades, like my son, can be squashed by educators who deem their knowledge in those arenas to be less than valuable. We know that the wide-ranging literacies—emotional, digital, popular culture, visual, lyrical—of kids of color are more often ignored to focus on "school" literacy. Dominant literacy. Often, less authentic literacy (Haddix and Sealey-Ruiz 2012).

I know that this can feel messy. It's hard to relinquish control. It's hard to let kids lead. There will be more classroom noise, more questions, and more days without tidy answers. But there's a big yield in

*Social literacies of fourth graders on the playground in Jersey City.*

giving kids more space to be curious, to follow what they love, and to make their own choices. Which learning produces bolder, more ingenious results: the cut-and-paste skyscraper template or the random popsicle sticks, toothpicks, and glue alongside images of buildings, allowing for kids to dream? Which offers space for safe failure: the fill-in-the-blank, write-as-I-say essay or the one that supports kids defending their own positions mightily because they're actually passionate about a topic? Which teaches students how to transfer what they learn out of the classroom to real life: the schooled literacy that dictates what, exactly, they should create or the one that asks what they're truly compelled to make as a result of their learning? Our parameter-setting and meticulously scaffolded project plans sometimes stifle children's imaginations. Kids rise far beyond what we imagine they can achieve as adults.

This does not mean that we hand ALL the power over to children tomorrow. They need our guidance. When it feels uncomfortable for teachers to give students free reign to choose their topics for learning, I encourage them to offer at least a few choices: this animal or that one? This weather phenomenon or that one? I recall when my son, in fourth grade, lamented that he needed to write an informational piece for class about squirrels. "Why don't you ask your teacher if you can research and write about predators, which I know you love?" I asked him. "No way, she won't budge," he responded. "Everyone *has to* write about squirrels." I thought about how much more passionate Ehsan would be about informational writing if he had been given a choice of topic to study and then share about. Any place for students to make decisions about their learning and thinking is critically important to their engagement. In these ways, children *are* the curriculum, if you allow them to pursue their own interests—even within simple parameters.

As a mother, I observed Ezzy's natural curiosity with energy and intrigue. I wanted to give her space and time to learn more about her personal interests, be that clouds or ice cream. As an educator, I recognize the importance of these same types of sparks for learning. But sometimes, when life and schedules and responsibilities weigh heavy on my shoulders, I fall back into rote and didactic thinking, both as a mother and as an educator—the mother who is harried and stressed about work and getting food on the table; the educator who needs to accomplish a lot each week to keep up with too many mandates. No doubt you often feel the same way. In moments like this, I try to remind myself to:

◈ Pause and take a deep breath

◈ Ask myself what matters most

◈ Center the children

In this way, we circle back to the truth that our children's engagement and interest in learning skyrocket when they get to choose their course of study, ways of sharing their learning, and modes of communication. Like adults, nobody wants to be told what to do for the sake of doing.

How can we ensure our young people feel that they have control and decision-making power in their own lives? If we don't want fill-in-the-blank kids, then we must establish instructional routines and practices that allow them to follow their natural, curious dispositions, and it's equally important that we communicate this mindset to caregivers (see Figure 6.1).

Giving kids choices across their days need not be a massive endeavor, but instead, a mindset for how caregivers generally operate. Our children have such little say in their days. Their schedules are often determined based on the needs of the family; their food options are limited, and they don't always choose what they wear. To give them agency over their lives, caregivers often give options whenever possible, however small or large, as their daily situation allows. *Do you want to wear these pants or those?* In our house, we have a visual that represents the options for a protein, starch, snack, and fruits and vegetables so each child can choose their lunch items based on the options we give them. I have found as a mother that my kids fare better and our days move more smoothly when I give them choices over something as simple as the order of how things will happen. *Do you want to bathe first or have dinner? Would you prefer to take a walk together first or run errands with me? Do you want me to read* The Blur *by Mihn Lê or* Octopus Stew *by Eric Velasquez? Do you want to go to the library before or after stopping by Abuela's?*

> If we don't want fill-in-the-blank kids, then we must establish instructional routines and practices that allow for them to follow their natural, curious dispositions, and it's equally important that we communicate this mindset to caregivers.

## Ways Choice Shows Up in Our Classrooms

When I think about my students' caregivers, I know so many of them likely grew up in an era and environment where choice was not central to their educational careers—or perhaps not an option at all. I think about my own parents being taught in Iran in the 1960s, where seats were assigned in rows and absolutely no choices were offered when it came to what was studied and how assignments looked. However different the learning environments may have been for our caregivers, in a holistic literacy classroom today, we value choice and know it to be critically important to engage students in culturally nourishing ways while also ensuring they can show up wholly with interest in our curricular planning. These elements of choice might not be immediately clear to caregivers, but they are hallmarks of a rich literacy learning experience.

**FIGURE 6.1**
*Choice-Focused Instruction to Clarify with Caregivers*

| Literacy Classroom Practice | What Might Not Be Clear to Caregivers |
|---|---|
| Choice in seating | Students, like adults, need to be comfortable to learn. Kids need to be able to self-determine whether they need a quiet spot, or whether they would benefit from collaborating with a peer. Can we offer flexible seating or a location that will allow for maximum comfort? Can we cultivate classrooms where students are able to make decisions throughout the day about where they might learn best? This might include the type of seating (beanbag, swivel stool, or stand-up desk) or the ability to move in various spaces in the classroom. I always tell families and students that when the bum is numb, so is the brain, because movement, too, is imperative for our brains to function well. I share with them the research that a lack of movement is akin to putting our brains in sleep mode. It might not be immediately clear to families why our classrooms—regardless of student age—might include these sorts of flexible options when it comes to space and body positioning, or how doing so increases student agency and autonomy in their learning experiences. |
| Choice in writing topics and modes | In what ways can we offer students choice over not only their writing topics but even the genre or mode they choose to communicate in? It may not be clear at all to caregivers that students might write about different topics that are of interest to them, or that they might be able to choose parts of writing that they want to work on for a grade. Because many of our caregivers might have come from more didactic literacy experiences, the value of choice based on interest might not be immediately accessible. Share with families that levels of engagement increase when students are able to choose what they research, write, and share. |
| Choice in assessment | Caregivers will want to know that in grades three through eight, we may ask students to choose the components of their writing that they want to be graded on, based on what they can show as evidence of growth. This type of personal selection for assessment also encourages student reflection, leading them to make clear improvements in their writing over time. |

FIGURE 6.1 *(continued)*

| Literacy Classroom Practice | What Might Not Be Clear to Caregivers |
|---|---|
| Choice in reading | Again, if caregivers don't have experiences with independent reading themselves, they might not realize that choice reading is a key factor in growing readers beyond classroom walls. Because rote textbook reading alongside comprehension questions may have been the core mode of teaching for caregivers in their own literacy experiences, it will take some explanation to communicate how important it is to allow students to read graphic novels, to reread books, to abandon books, and to partner-read. |
| Choice in artifact | Recognizing the critical importance of giving students choices in how they share their thinking *after* reading might be the most shocking for caregivers coming from traditional education spaces. We might ask kids, *what did this reading compel you to create? What do you want your peers to know about what you just read? How do you want to show off your thinking? What did you just learn that you want to share with the world? What is the best way for you to share it?* Likely, you use a reading menu of multimodal options for sharing thinking after independent reading that includes everything from building to creating to writing to recording to video options—all valid and important forms of expression. This choice work isn't relegated to reading alone. When applied to writing, we might ask students, *how will your final product look when you go to publish it? What have you read that's like what you're envisioning?* Caregivers need to hear from classroom teachers that these are valid options and each decision is part of the child's individual growth. |

These aren't the only ways to offer choice in the classroom, of course. To encourage students' flexibility and spontaneity and to show the ways that we are varied, textured, and different in our thinking, learning, and sharing tendencies, we can continue to brainstorm places in our literacy blocks where choices can be offered. If you are a school leader, I urge you to intentionally pause periodically to leave space for educators to reflect on choice. In fact, I hope you'll leave room for educators to *choose*, too, the ways they want to grow and which professional learning opportunities they want to invest in. In one of my classrooms, students decide whether they want to join in on small groups around additional conferring lessons to elevate their writing. They can sign up for the small group, or they can choose to work independently. Or they can choose to move to the "peer partner" space, where they can seek feedback on a specific part of writing. In other class-rooms, students might choose to lead their peers in small groups when the teacher identifies a strength in their writing. Not dissimilar to a small-group conference, I've seen students in fourth grade and beyond share their expert writing moves with friends during independent work time, which creates a sense of pride and ownership over what they know and do well. These additional choices for students continually communicate that they are in control of various aspects of their learning; that they have a voice; that they have agency; that the classroom is crafted *for* them and *by* them. Like a textured kilim, it communicates a stance of collective consideration for each individual's ways of being.

# More Ways to Explore the Power of Choice

Sharing learning experiences while exploring a variety of resources will always be one of the best ways families can support the power of choice. Here are a few favorites to keep the conversation going with kids, caretakers, and educators.

| Text Title | Author |
| --- | --- |
| *My Fade Is Fresh* (2022) | Shauntay Grant |
| *Hands* (2023) | Torrey Maldonado |
| *Tumble* (2022) | Celia C. Pérez |
| *Amal Unbound* (2018) and *Omar Rising* (2022) | Aisha Saeed |
| *Magic Has No Borders* (2023) | Edited by Sona Charaipotra and Samira Ahmed |
| *Another Appalachia: Coming Up Queer and Indian in a Mountain Place* (2022) | Neema Avaisha |

## Elevating

One of the best ways to elevate choice in student learning experiences at school is with projects that aim to exalt the nourishing components of authentic learning and that take reading, writing, thinking, and talking beyond school-based activities alone. We can create robust literacy experiences when students connect to the world; when students can see their curiosities lead to learning; when students realize their learning can lead to change, collaborative care, and nourishment. Although not every family will have time to engage in big projects outside of school, we must share ideas with families for generating opportunities to read, write, talk, and think together, all while giving students space to choose or follow their natural curiosities. When kids inevitably show interest in the world around them, we can find natural places to elevate literacy learning.

For example, when my friend's sixth-grade daughter was briefly obsessed with clothing brands, she suggested they research more about company practices for how the clothing was made. Together with her daughter, they searched for information on the slow fashion movement. They learned about low wages and unfair labor laws in other countries until they decided as a family to commit to solely purchasing repurposed or equitably made clothing—online, on Instagram, or from second-hand shops—in a stand against harmful practices of business conglomerates. Her daughter even wrote a letter to her friends to explain why *not* to contribute to inequitable practices, complete with examples of where to purchase (and swap) reused clothes.

In another instance, my son's friend took it upon himself to learn extensively about unihemispheric behaviors of birds after his father said "Sleep is for the birds," wanting to discover what the phrase really meant. Though it's a commonly used idiom, what he learned is that birds sometimes sleep with only half of their brains, with the other half awake at the very same time. This is authentic literacy connected to choice.

Mishay Patel, a classmate of my daughter's in Jersey City, makes simple coding videos with his father that they post on YouTube. "It was more about following what he was interested in learning," his dad told me. "Instead of us saying you should learn this or that, we let him choose, and it's a good thing for me to spend time with him."

The natural invitations are cultivated by families and their children, where their curiosities are followed into real learning. Because not all families will readily think of these sorts of learning roadways, we might communicate these ideas as a starting off point.

## Bigger Bridges Between Home and School: The Neighborhood Critical Lens Project

Some suggestions for family literacy projects can be more involved, especially if they're still driven by student choice. A handful of my schools participate in incredibly rich summer literacy projects that involve multistep connections between caregivers and the home. They begin close to the end of the academic year with reminders throughout the summer and often feature a fall showcase upon return to school. What I call the Neighborhood Critical Lens Project supports students and their caregivers in working together to look around their communities for inequities and issues they want to learn more about. This practice not only builds the cultural competence of teachers but simultaneously allows for students and their families to critically examine the world around them—something they are often already naturally doing. But it all starts from children's personal choices about what they see and are curious about, so they can lead their learning alongside caregivers throughout the summer. Through conversations with caregivers and the turning of a critical eye toward neighborhoods and communities we live in, students can recognize issues and trends that they might want to then learn more about, starting with three main critical lens questions:

◈ What privileges do I notice?

◈ What inequalities do I see?

◈ Who benefits from this trend in my neighborhood?

For example, students at our schools noticed changes happening in Chicago's Humboldt Park neighborhood over time. They noticed new stores popping up, with more expensive coffee, and boutique shops selling "fancy" housewares. The critical lens questions led them to important conversations with their caregivers about gentrification. The resources this group looked at included analyzing the Chicago gentrification and displacement map via the Urban Displacement Project, interviewing the owner of a local florist who had been there for decades, and researching the two enormous Puerto Rican flags made of steel that denote the neighborhood's rich cultural history as a means of standing against gentrification. This literacy learning stemmed from their own choices and allowed for conversation that explored the pros and cons of neighborhood change.

*Humboldt Park, Chicago.*

## THE ENCOURAGEMENT OF FREEDOM DOES NOT MEAN THE LOSS OF CONTROL

"She's a good teacher, because her class is always under control." How often have we heard this? "That family is a good family because their children are so quiet." School has a perplexing history of silencing children and then celebrating the oppressive victory of that act.

Talk when I say talk. Move when I say move. Use the bathroom only when I allow it.

The presence of this kind of "order" ensures only one kind of learning. Kids learn to find self-worth in pleasing authority, and they delay learning to find it in themselves. No one wants this for their young people, yet in too many communities, allowing children to exercise freedom is often associated with being a lackadaisical parent or an ineffective teacher.

Though many of us grew up in schools and homes with few choices as young people, we can help communities to work toward a different kind of order. Classroom "discipline" built on a foundation of choice, accountability, and collective responsibility grows learning and LIVING that is richer than "order" built on punishment, fear, and unexamined obedience. This is true for home, too. To learn more, read Dr. Robin D. G. Kelly's *Freedom Dreams: The Black Radical Imagination* (2003).

The purpose of this project was to offer choice in continued summer learning, but it became so much more than that. Caregivers reported that their students talked to them more, opened their eyes more, and asked questions they then sought answers to together. When everyone returned to school in August, teachers were able to group students based on similar topic interests or conduct a more traditional showcase of the summer projects for all kids to hear and learn. In the case of students studying gentrification, teachers shared picture books like *Alejandria Fights Back! La Lucha de Alejandria!* (2021) by Leticia Hernandez-Linares and the *Rise-Home Stories Project* (www.risehomestories.com) for further authentic engagement. My favorite young adult and adult reads that grapple with gentrification right now are *When We Make It* (2021) by Elisabet Velasquez, *Olga Dies Dreaming* (2022) by Xochitl Gonzalez, and *Neruda on the Park* (2022) by Cleyvis Natera.

# Elevating Caregiver Involvement Around Choice

| If you're focusing on . . . at school . . . | Caregivers might . . . |
| --- | --- |
| Choosing independent work spots thoughtfully | Give their children more leeway when it comes to making decisions about where they do their homework or when, engaging in conversations afterward about what went right and what didn't as a result. |
| Increasing student engagement during independent work time, offering choices for small-group topics or activities | Offer a greater degree of choice in downtimes for the family, and offer decision-making points throughout the day for how the schedule might look. They might make space for their children to brainstorm interests and follow them, for example, a local museum exhibit or a visit to a specific playground. |
| Student choice in writing modality, allowing children to decide what mode of writing best communicates their messages | Point to different modes of writing in the real world—advertisements, signs, commercials, billboards, pamphlets in the doctor's office—that communicate a message. They might ask questions about why that modality works or doesn't, and what might be better for communicating the point. |
| Diversifying the classroom library options | Brainstorm with their children topics they want to learn more about or talk about stories they wish existed in the world, so that students can share their ideas with their classroom teachers. If kids are already talking with their caregivers about what they want to learn, they'll be better equipped to make choices in the classroom that amplify their agency. |

## Inviting

Because our kids are naturally interested in the world around them—mostly based on what they see, hear, and experience—it is a fun exercise to make a list of topics they're interested in and request books about those topics from the local children's librarian. The library holds queue is one of our most heavily relied-on entertainment and learning structures. These days, most of the topics my children brainstorm are animals, so they come home after our weekly library trip with books on hamsters, dogs, and other cuddly options as part of their parental plea to get a pet. Because we saw baby turtles being sold on the sidewalk at Coney Island, Eloisa asked for a book on "tortugas." They even spent some time discussing the differences in the books based on the years they were published, because some of the texts were from the '80s ("Mom, this was printed when YOU were born!")—a discussion that sprung quite naturally without my prompting.

We always make friends with our local librarians, especially the ones who work so hard to honor reader choices. In both Chicago and Jersey City, Shirley and Quae know my children's interests—and keep up with them—more than any other adult can keep up. They'll put new books aside for my kids as they come in, like *Dory Fantasmagory* by Abby Hanlon for Eloisa because she chatters incessantly about calling the characters on a banana (a detail of the series). They'll pull cookbooks for Eliana. They'll have the new Marvel title checked out under Ehsan's card because they know what he likes. Libraries are my most treasured choice-yielding resource. We can be more like librarians. They "read" kids (with observational literacy skills; see Chapter 4) to develop an understanding of who they are, and then they act on what they know, trusting that not every action will be a perfect match, but every action will communicate to a child that there is somebody here who sees you and is committed to the person that they know that you can be (even if you are not being that person right now).

*Children can lead their learning.*

This is what educators want for their students. This is what caregivers want for their children. We can support parents on this journey. We can deliver this.

## Considerations for Inviting Caregivers to Elevate Choice with Their Children

Every family is different, but if we communicate with caregivers about why choice is important and where we can bring some degree of decision-making power for kids into the home, we widen opportunity and possibility for students to feel further seen and heard. When children have the ability to make decisions based on their personal preferences, adults communicate that their opinions are important and valid.

Caregivers can continue to offer choices for children in intentional ways, including but not limited to:

◈ Choice over what children wear, leaning into freedom of expression that allows them to feel comfortable and supported in finding their style.

◈ Choice in the order of operations about scheduling: this first, or that?

◈ Choice in learning spaces: where they'll do homework and in what order they'll work, including a discussion about when they feel most focused.

◈ Choice in pursuing interests, ranging from activities to book topics to television.

◈ Choice in how the table is set, how a room looks, what goes on the walls— all safe spaces for children to feel empowered to make decisions based on their own personal preferences, excitement, and desires.

◈ Choice in how a free weekend day or afternoon might go, allowing for "yes" days that result in children choosing whether they want to visit a specific park, museum, or friend.

A few mornings ago, before the children came to the kitchen, I turned on Oxlade's "KU LO SA," a song I've loved recently. I poured myself a cup of coffee. I opened the front blinds to the street. These are all choices I made because they're my preferences, ones that make me content and happy. I like to start mornings with upbeat songs, and I like my coffee black and piping hot. I like to observe the city as it jostles awake, with sun streaming through the front window. I am an adult; I get to make these choices—not unlike the countless caregivers we work with every day. But children don't always have a chance to craft these preferences in their days. Much of what they do is lumped into what has to be done, in community with others. But the "because I said so" of my own childhood doesn't feel like the right line anymore, not as a caregiver. And it doesn't have to be that way in the classroom, either. As we center choice making in nourishing ways that allow for children to be fully themselves and engage more thoroughly, they will flourish in our care.

> But the "because I said so" of my own childhood doesn't feel like the right line anymore, not as a caregiver. And it doesn't have to be that way in the classroom, either.

# Reflecting: Choice: Freeing Students to Make Self-Driven Decisions

| | |
|---|---|
| **Brainstorm all the ways a child might have choice in their home lives. How might you build on those to offer similar choices in your classroom?** | **In what ways are you already offering choice in your classroom? Which of those practices can be enhanced? Which are ready to be refined?** |
| | |
| **What suggestions might you make to caregivers to offer greater choice for their children? What shared literacy values can be communicated with families about offering moments for more choice, both at school and at home?** | **List some of the choices you have the privilege of deciding among as an adult. Think about children in those moments and what choices they aren't invited to make. Are there any places we can give children, in those moments, some agency?** |
| | |
| **Think about a specific child who tends to resist flexibility and spontaneity in your classroom. How can you teach choice as a tool for the student to increase power over their own learning journey?** | **Think about your literacy block. List the components you include across a given week. For each part, add a choice you might offer students in an effort to strengthen independence and agency.** |
| | |

## Reflection Space

Feel free to use this additional space to process the reflection
questions and your own thinking from this chapter.

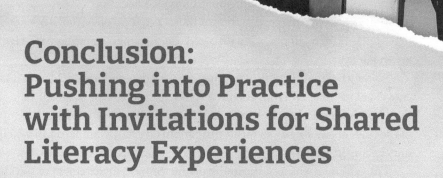

# Conclusion:
# Pushing into Practice
# with Invitations for Shared
# Literacy Experiences

Imagine a classroom with a teacher—me—kneeling in front of a group of kindergarten students seated nearby on the rug with their caregivers huddled beside them. Together, we're looking at an image on screen of my toddler hiding behind a bunch of hanging winter coats. Her face is not visible, but her tiny feet are.

"Hello, my friends," I start, grinning widely. I pause purposefully for the host teacher to translate my words into Spanish, then start again, speaking slowly.

"This is a photo of my daughter. She is four years old. And she is very silly."

I stop dramatically, smiling wide.

"Do you want to learn more about her?" Eager heads bounce up and down. The caregivers are smiling, too. Most of them are touching their children lovingly, with just a hand to steadily communicate their presence.

"One way that you can learn more about something is by reading an image and asking yourself, what do you see, notice, and wonder," I say, pointing to my eyes, then lifting my hands in an inquisitive manner. I point to three icons that denote see (eyes), notice (magnifying glass), and wonder (question mark) on a nearby chart.

I continue by modeling how to ask questions about Eloisa and her behavior and draw conclusions about what I now know about her by reading the image.

"Do you want to read more about Eloisa?" I ask.

I share another image, this time of Eloisa standing on a stool while tending to potted plants on a windowsill with a red, duck-shaped watering can. Her bangs are in her eyes.

As they begin discussing what they see, wonder, and notice, I lean into family conversations, encouraging them to speak in Spanish or English, or a mix of the two—however they feel most comfortable. I have a baby on my hip—one of the students' siblings—as I lead this family labsite; I want it to feel welcoming, underplanned, and joyful.

I'm extremely enthusiastic and truly fueled by the excitement of the children and their caregivers, all analyzing images together. After the "we do" portion of this family labsite, I pass out color copies of pictures from children's books set in Los Angeles, where these kindergarten students would have neighborhood context and familiarity. Together with their families, they talk about what they see, notice, and wonder as they read the images from the books.

At the end of the twenty-minute shared literacy experience, we gather, and I emphasize for families that reading images *is* in fact reading and that we can encourage children to read the world as we move about our regular days at home. I hold up a small bag of Cheez-Its and ask, "What do you see, notice, and wonder?" Opportunities for environmental literacy practice are everywhere. We can read anything in our paths. This is building the same critical thinking skills we aim to teach in a literacy classroom.

Across Chapters 2 through 6, we've considered ways to infuse powerful home literacy practices into our classrooms and vice versa. In this final chapter, we'll expand from there as we explore how we can work directly with families and schools to collaborate in ways that stay rooted to a holistic and compassionate ethic of collective care. It all begins with attention to three critical details:

◈ **Take time** to grapple with what we believe makes up a family, leaving space to excavate our biases about how families should look, act, and engage. In these initial stages, it's important caregivers feel safe to bring their full selves into our spaces so their colleagues and schools can see, feel, and hear all of them.

◈ **Identify** places across the year where you can invite families into your classrooms and shared school spaces. As you do, be cognizant of family work schedules and the ways you invite them in. This shouldn't feel stressful and can be as simple as asking families to come for a shared literacy experience with their children.

◈ **Review your curriculum** and brainstorm with colleagues places where you can *listen, honor, connect, elevate,* or *invite* families in direct ways that overlap your already-existing units of study. Engaging in this purposeful planning and reflection with colleagues often means embedding spaces throughout our curricular planning as reminders to ask ourselves at every juncture: is this a place where I could exalt a family experience or cultivate a caregiver collaboration?

## FAMILY LABSITES

The work in this chapter builds largely on my firsthand experiences running family labsites for caregivers and communities. A family labsite is simply an invitation for caregivers to come into a communal space to share in a literacy experience alongside their children. Labsites can be large or small, held on school grounds or in community settings, and can be offered at times that are most convenient for family members and offer the highest potential for engagement. If you're interested in embedding family labsite experiences into your work with caregivers, all you need is to invite families to come in for shared time (twenty or thirty minutes works!) with their children. Model a strategy of any kind. Allow kids to try it out with their caregivers. Circulate and encourage. Reveal an authentic desire to connect with families.

As you plan your own family labsite experiences, you'll want to keep the Collective Care Framework (described on page 167) in mind. Most of all, it's just about nourishing caregivers by setting up mini and replicable experiences to read, write, draw, talk, and problem-solve alongside their children. Think of it as a low-stakes, collaborative learning session.

*Family labsite in a kindergarten classroom, Los Angeles.*

Families and caregivers are the essential connective tissue in learning experiences for children, because they provide fodder for curiosity, springboards for critical conversation and emotional literacy, and generational knowledge that is essential for growing children toward a more equitable society. Historically, family engagement has looked and sounded like schools telling families what to do and how to do it, with the intention of children doing school "well." But in the family literacy research I've been invested in for years, I've learned that this model doesn't serve us, our students, or our caregivers.

**Engaging in this purposeful planning and reflection with colleagues often means embedding spaces throughout our curricular planning as reminders to ask ourselves at every juncture: is this a place where I could exalt a family experience or cultivate a caregiver collaboration?**

With these three concepts grounding our mindset, I propose a new framework that first elevates the authentic and wholly valuable, literacy-rich ways that families are already sharing reading, writing, thinking, and problem-solving with their children. Bringing those experiences into the classroom, via either small or large invitations, we exalt the family experience and increase student engagement, which folds families into the instructional promise of student learning. This creates a cycle of nourishing, collective care. It doesn't happen overnight, nor is there a one-size-fits-all approach to family literacy work. It cannot be a workbook; it cannot be a single tear-sheet meant to stick on the fridge. What we know is that events like one-off literacy nights do not sustain change. We also know that we cannot separate knowing our students from knowing their families. We must build relationships and strong communication methods with each and every one; we must breathe in a pedagogical stance of positivity and asset-based behaviors no matter who the families are, or what sort of upbringing we had ourselves.

In all my research for family literacy engagement in Chicago, including school interviews and the connections I've made to Los Angeles and East Coast communities since then through ongoing family literacy labsites, I have identified several important factors to consider when executing strong family literacy engagement opportunities. As you close this book and turn your attention toward inviting families further into your spaces and work, consider these findings, which stem directly from my conversations with stakeholders in over a dozen pilot schools and culminate in a nourishing blueprint I've come to call the Collective Care Framework. This framework serves to engage families in meaningful and collaborative experiences that are respectful, inclusive, and sustainable. As you read through the components of the framework that follows, think about where your own school's engagement practices align or could use additional texture and revision (see the Synthesizing the Collective Care Framework reflection template in Appendix B).

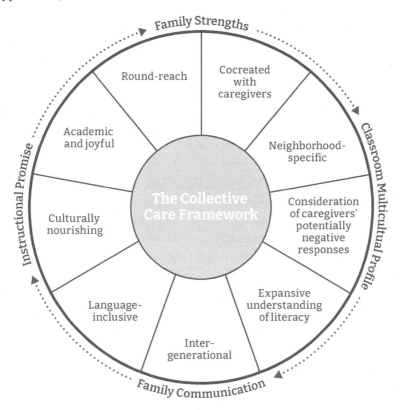

## Effective Family Engagement Programs Are Academic and Joyful

Family literacy programming across time should be engaging, playful, and joyous while, at the same time, sharing academic content and looping caregivers into current classroom practices for teaching reading and writing. Of course, caregivers will want to know what the curriculum is like, what expectations are being set for students, and how their children are moving toward growth. But in the family literacy labsites I've facilitated, the practice of shared, fun literacy experience is the first step in engaging caregivers in our work. For example, in a fourth-grade family labsite, caregivers coconstructed neighborhood maps with their children, drawing where they live and some hallmarks of what surrounds them: bodegas and food stands, libraries, parks, train and bus stops, and so on. You can't help but marvel at the powerful practice of caregivers and their children passing markers back and forth, telling stories about moments they remember from each of the spots they draw, laughing when a cat looks hilariously lopsided, solemnly questioning where it was that police gathered when a window was once shattered. First and foremost, we center the joy inherent in the collaborative experience of coconstructing between children and their caregivers, and, afterward, we explain the brainstorming strategy they engaged in as part of the writing process and finding moments of emotion connected to place as a writerly move for story-building.

"It was the joy for me," said one teacher in a labsite debrief, after observing caregivers with their children. "All I could see were their smiles."

## Strong Family Engagement Programs Are Culturally Nourishing

At the start of this book's journey, we considered the internal work we must do to ensure that we aren't perpetuating stereotypes and biases we all inevitably carry because of how we were raised. All families look different, and each child's caregivers bring their own educational and familial experiences to the ways they think about school, so we want to take extra care to avoid alienating anyone when we invite families into our work. To build toward cultural sustainability in our classrooms and with families, we must ask questions, read extensively, and empathize with the experiences of caregivers. We must acknowledge, validate, and encourage each person's ways of being.

One activity I've led with educators to reflect on getting to know families better is to brainstorm on one side of a three-column chart the names of students whose families they don't know much about. In the middle column, I ask teachers to list the questions they have. And in the last column, I ask, *How might you get there?* We then brainstorm as colleagues how we might find answers to the questions, thinking as compassionately and gently as we can about all the potential barriers to our understanding. This exercise is a beautiful way to work toward getting to know the whole child, because knowing our students is inextricably intertwined with knowing their caregivers. With some reflection, educators often notice that biases tend to percolate in the middle column, when brainstorming what they wish they knew. *What motivates the child at home? Who prepares the meals? How is the child spoken to? How is the child loved?* The mere act of thinking through these questions helps teachers plan family engagement more thoughtfully, in ways that are more culturally sensitive and encompassing diversity in all aspects of the word. Family events and integrated experiences across the year should honor the rich legacies of all backgrounds, to exalt the already-established complexities of our student communities.

## Family Literacy Experiences
## Must Be Language Inclusive

Every aspect of family literacy engagement needs to include biliteracy if your families are speaking more than one language. Use every tool imaginable to translate flyers, emails, and messages, and be sure to have a translator (parent volunteers are often honored to help out). Because we are working to break down barriers instead of creating more, we must believe there are no "home" language and "school" languages when it comes to family engagement. Rather, *all* languages are welcome and encouraged, heritage languages are embraced, and all of our communication must reflect that belief. Translation, in the case of family engagement, should be viewed more as an elimination of communication barriers. For instance, I speak Farsi and some Spanish, some Arabic, and some French, but not much more in those three languages beyond introductions. But I communicate with my hand on my chest. Through the children. With drawings. With other adults who can help. In what ways can we ensure that families know language will not be the dividing line between school and home? This takes intentionality; big, open hearts, and wide, purposeful smiles (despite our long to-do lists) that communicate to all families that they are an integral part of their child's schooling and education.

## Intergenerational Experiences
## Are Essential to Family Engagement

Because we need all families to participate, we don't want childcare to become an issue or a sticking point when planning literacy events and family labsites. Encourage intergenerational support by reminding those with small children that they can bring their entire family system: babies, grandparents, cousins, or otherwise. If you feel young kids might be a distraction in a shared family literacy experience, set up an alternate table in the space with coloring or board books that might briefly entertain young ones, or brainstorm some intentional ways you might include the entire family in the fun. In some of the most successful family labsites I've led, teachers have found that older siblings want to show off or share with younger kids what they're learning. They're not new to sharing space or juggling younger siblings, and there's an element of pride in sharing their classroom experiences.

When considering timing for events, keep scheduling in mind as well: caregiver work hours, schedules for other children in the family, one parent with too many places to be, mealtimes, transportation, and more. Which of these barriers can we eliminate by scheduling labsites and shared literacy experiences at a variety of times, such as just after morning drop-off or in the evenings? I am often parenting solo two or three days a week, and it is impossible for me to juggle all of the children's school events, because I am not an octopus—but that doesn't make me a disengaged parent. Over and over I tell folks: bring your babies—mine might be there. All are welcome.

## An Expansive Understanding of Literacy Must Honor the Gifts Families Bring

Literacy learning cannot be separated from the interpersonal, contextualized meaning-making that occurs every day between caregivers and their children. Although phonics and foundational skills are absolutely essential, when my doctor asks how she should teach her son how to read, especially because he speaks Mandarin to her parents and English to everyone else, I tell her what I know, deep in my bones: communicate with him naturally.

"Does it matter if he can articulate which letters match which sounds, at this point?" she asks me, while I'm up on the table in my gown.

I smile. "He'll get there. In the meantime, tell stories. Narrate everything. Ask questions together."

She worries about which language he uses, when. I assure her that it doesn't matter. I tell her he can toggle between Mandarin and English; he can choose to pepper in words in each or use whatever language he has in his repertoire. She worries that he watches too much TV; I tell her to pause it periodically and ask questions to chat about afterward.

"Did you know that kid's television shows with characters who pause and ask the audience questions have educational consultants?" I ask her.

My doctor looks relieved. Every caregiver worries in their own ways. My short conversation with her explaining the expansive definition of literacy we must consider to grow our children's critical thinking minds helped her understand how to better support her little learner. It's what we must do for all families in our care.

## Hold Space for Potentially Negative Education Experiences of Caregivers

It is no surprise that some caregivers come to us with less than positive experiences with schools and education spaces from when they were growing up. Check yourself now and flip back to the start of this book, where we consider the biases we all carry when it comes to how "engaged" families should look, sound, and act. I think about one of my best friends, who has never read a book all the way through, who was taught in a self-contained special education classroom, who has worked for years in telecommunications, first as a "cable guy" in New Jersey and now maintaining Internet in lower Manhattan. Here's a hardworking man who never felt successful at school himself.

"How am I supposed to know what to do for my kid?" he asks me. "I've gotta trust the teachers."

The reality of potential generational trauma or feelings of low confidence, perpetuated in part by inequitable systems in our schools, must be handled with care. Not all parents had solid experiences with formal education. Many parents feel they can't support their kids because they themselves were not seen or heard in their traditional, often arcane school systems. Those insecurities must be acknowledged and treated with unbiased consideration.

## An Understanding of Communities and Neighborhoods Elevates Family Engagement Opportunities

The Pilsen neighborhood of Chicago is one of my favorites and one of the most vibrant. Its inhabitants are mostly Mexican. It's home to the National Museum of Mexican Art. Brightly colored murals appear on every other corner, and Spanish music can be heard at all hours; they arguably have the best tacos in the city, with homemade corn tortillas and guacamole, with more lime and cilantro than most restaurants. People who live and work in Pilsen and know it intimately do a better job of understanding the children and families in it, and when the school system understands, honors, and celebrates these details that make Pilsen unique, they're situated to more effectively support the families that live there.

"Living in and knowing the neighborhood makes a huge difference," commented one of my school principals. "When they know the neighborhood, they know the needs."

That's why schools that partner with local organizations that support family book access, classes, or event planning are better positioned to collaborate seamlessly. Whether the organizations offer cooking classes, family outings, or something else, if they are local and neighborhood-specific, they often better understand the needs of the community. One of my Chicago schools, for example, partners with Vocel, a nonprofit based in the city that strengthens early learning in homes, schools, and communities. Because Vocel intimately understands the landscape of Chicago neighborhoods, they're better equipped to know what to offer families. They offer Zumba, knitting, technology, and ESL classes for the Chavez school community because their liaisons know that's what Back of the Yards families need. Andres Avila, a longtime counselor in Chicago Public Schools, underscored the importance of this level of community intimacy: "Just the practice of seeing where kids live, what their block looks like, what it feels like walking down that street—just to give teachers more context about where kids are coming from. It says a lot to a kid."

## Cocreating with Caregivers Supports Sustainability

As you might imagine, as with all things, the most sustainable programs are designed by the people involved in them. Like community organizer and activist Mariame Kaba learned from her father, "everything worthwhile is done with others" (Kaba 2021). When parents and caregivers cocreate and make decisions about opportunities for engaging with their children and school—determining what events look like, deciding what books to collaboratively read and discuss, directing questions of educators to better understand the literacy landscape of the school—programs are more likely to stick. As you work to give caregivers further agency and confidence in supporting their students in the long term, consider inviting them into the planning process, either individually or as committees. Not only does doing so create an inviting, welcoming mindset, but families often know better what will be most successful within their communities and what will resonate most effectively with caregivers. This is no different from any sort of organizational learning: when the stakeholders are involved, there's increased engagement, interest, and genuine change.

## A Holistic Vision for Nourishing Caregiver Collaborations Includes a Round-Reach Mentality

Finally, though each of these suggestions is equally important for a collective and nourishing effort of collaborative care, no single component of this framework will carry a strong family literacy engagement program alone. Nor will our efforts be sustainable over time without what I call a round-reach. When I say round-reach, I mean wraparound care that encompasses a recognition of all the ways that families contribute uniquely and all the different levels of support they need. I mean considerations about book access and communicating children's growth process; I mean embracing the wisdom of our students' elders into the ways we breathe life into teaching. I mean remembering that joy is not just a buzzword but a way of being with and for our children and their families—recognizing all the struggles and daily challenges families face; imagining their nuanced histories.

Meaningful, sustainable home-school connections are rooted in this type of compassion. When the Collective Care Framework is grounded in a robust roundreach system, each of its elements increasingly builds toward more nourishing collaborations with caregivers that will raise instructional promise, elevating opportunities for families to feel integral to their children's educational journeys.

The challenging process of writing a book about involving families more wholly and authentically in school systems has been the direct result of my own journey to become a more compassionate human. To give myself and others grace. To be more understanding. To be softer, but also fiercely committed to my beliefs. To listen more. And to push breath into the parts that feel really hard. Carla Shalaby, in her book *Troublemakers: Lessons in Freedom from Young Children at School*, writes, "I care about the lives of children at school because I am an educator, and as an educator, it is my job to insist on every child's right to a classroom experience that honors her, reveres her smarts, engages her curiosities, and ensures her dignity" (2017). These lessons in freedom extend to families.

My time spent in schools as I wrote only validated what I've known in my heart all along: that exceptional teachers are exceptional because they love so hard, that, like poet Alexis Pauline Gumbs says in conversation with Adrienne Marie Brown, "the possibilities of our living shift directly in relationship to the rigor of our loving" (2019). This is no different from exceptional nurses or exceptional drivers or exceptional journalists or exceptional bankers. It doesn't take fancy programs, and we don't need permission. It takes a commitment to collective care. To nourish ourselves, our profession, and ALL of our children, we must love their families hard, too. We must get to know them. Table judgment. Communicate consistently. Exude support. And trust the process, leaning into the places where collaboration with families feels hard. This is where our work is at its most genuine and authentic. Every school that engages in this work meaningfully finds new and better routes for collaboration. Connections that I can't even imagine. Because the ingenuity lies in *your* compassion, with *your* unique children and their families, year after year. We can do better. And we must.

> It doesn't take fancy programs, and we don't need permission. It takes a commitment to collective care. To nourish ourselves, our profession, and ALL of our children, we must love their families hard, too.

I want for all of my children's teachers to nurture, nourish, and collaborate with me and my family in these ways. I want this for *everyone's* children.

I hope that the ideas in this book have shown you that the ways to nourishing caregiver collaborations are limitless. And I hope your mind is aflame with ideas for how to take these dreams into our work, with all families.

The truth is, this book is a plea. It is a direct ask for you to join me in this journey to be and grow more compassionate humans.

When I was young, when I fell and scraped my knees, or if someone hurt my feelings, my mother would squeeze me and say, "Bozorg mishee yadet mire." It's something her mother told her and something my great-grandmother told my grandmother. It means "You'll grow older and forget." This Farsi phrase reminds us how quickly things pass. How time bends in the direction of adulthood. How, when we're small, everything feels important. This idea—you'll grow older and forget—carries with it a sense of urgency. We must keep this perspective of elderly wisdom in mind as we face the world each day for our children.

Pause. Reflect. Reimagine.

What matters most?

What will they grow old and *not* forget?

# Afterword

In *Nourishing Caregiver Collaborations*, Nawal captures
a humanistic, child- and caregiver-centered approach for
schools to show the ways they can deeply care for the whole
child and their village. The kilim serves as a metaphor for this
text in a remarkably fitting form, inviting us to engage with
Nawal's weaving of her learnings from mothering, teaching,
literacy coaching, and everyday life. In doing so, she reveals
intricate and intentional approaches for nurturing authentic
collaborations.

In reading this book, we couldn't help but think of
our initial connections with Nawal and how her words so
beautifully represent who she is at her very core. No doubt
you've sensed her genuine heart as you've read it as well.
During the pandemic, Nawal showed kindness in an online
world that can sometimes be disheartening. She supported
our debut book by crafting a thoughtful review, inviting others
to our book events, and showing genuine interest in the ways
we can offer support for bilingual and multilingual students
with her engagement and thought-provoking questions. Not
too long after, she sent something in the mail for Luz, and
because she learned that Luz had a son close in age to one of
her children, she also included her kids' hand-written letters

and drawings for her son. Luz's home has reminders of Nawal's thoughtfulness: a macrame wall hanging, a nazar—an amulet to ward off the "evil eye"— made from clay, and handwritten "thank you" cards that arrive after her visits. The times we've spent with Nawal talking about books and parenting, and connecting over the beauty and challenges of these paths we walk, have always left us recentered and eager to continue this important work together.

We share these personal stories to illustrate how Nawal *lives* and nourishes authentic connections. By sharing her stories woven throughout *Nourishing Caregiver Collaborations*, we see the different parts that make her whole. And in turn, reading this book invites us to similarly reflect on the crucial moments of our journey that continue to define us and make us whole. As her own words remind us, all of this, too, is a work in progress. Living and embodying what we share with the rest of the world (through any medium) is critical. Because if there is something we know for sure it is that children, families, and caregivers know and feel when our actions come from a place of authenticity, commitment, and love.

As scholars, we find ourselves drawn to Angela Valenzuela's (1999) critique of subtractive schooling. Her question resonates: How can we expect children to care about their education if they aren't shown that they, too, are cared for by their teachers? This notion reverberates deeply as we step into our roles as mothers, each navigating intricate relationships with our children's schools. We consider how inclusivity feels to us (fully aware of our privileges as education scholars and how even more so we need to listen) and the questions that arise.

We have also been the language brokers for our immigrant families, guiding them through the complexities of immigration, family separation, and learning a new culture and landscape. In this experience, the words of scholars like Suárez-Orozco, Suárez-Orozco, and Todorova (2010) in their book, *Learning a New Land: Immigrant Students in American Society*, resonate. We have lived through the intricate tapestry of emotions attached to the responsibility of guiding our loved ones on this journey, which we continue to do now into adulthood. We see our own experiences reflected in this book as we recognize the crucial role we have had and continue to have in constructing our families' experiences in the U.S. Reading how Nawal learns from her interactions with her family members gives us perspective and reminds us that this is an ongoing endeavor. How beautiful that we get these words in *Nourishing Caregiver Collaborations* to nurture our own family relationships and those of our students.

Today's socio-political landscape paints a picture where the narratives of families from the global majority are far from nourishing. We hear a harmful rhetoric across the country riddled with book bans and anti-truth campaigns, denying the humanity of all children. Our hearts ache as we witness the dehumanization of immigrant families at the Texas-Mexico border, their existence threatened by buoys and razor-wire fencing along the Rio Grande. Additionally, legislation across the U.S. disregards the voices of queer children, Black, Indigenous, and families of color by banning histories and books depicting their present experiences and struggles.

As teacher educators, we wonder how we can continue shaping future teachers that center family collaborations in ways Nawal thoughtfully describes. Something we feel more equipped and supported to do with Nawal's work.

Nawal's writing lays her vulnerability bare, revealing her whole self and past assumptions and biases. The journey presents teachable moments, not only for Nawal as a mother but also in her role as an educator and literacy coach. The nuances of Arab and Persian culture are rich, offering groundedness and space for critical examination, heeding the words of Sonia Nieto (1994), moving beyond the surface level of acceptance and into solidarity and critique. Nawal notes, "the conversations we have with caregivers today still reflect the same biases, assumptions, and concerns" (p. 21) unearthing a path to examining harmful narratives passed down through generations, making space for unlearning.

*Nourishing Caregiver Collaborations* prompts us to consider how these school-caregiver partnerships take shape in different communities. How might immigrant students and mixed-status families be supported? For instance, Nawal's text recommendations in each chapter offer entry points for those with limited access to family stories. More specifically, we can consider what we know about the current research on ways families are included in school life, particularly with populations like emergent bilinguals labeled as disabled (Cioè-Peña, 2021). Nawal recommends elevating the collective and listening deeply to children's processes instead of focusing on an end product—honoring the varied ways children learn. We also turn our attention to queer students and their chosen families. Nawal offers guidance to encourage a shift from traditional family trees, a common assignment in K–12 classrooms, toward embracing community maps. What's more, we reflect on what it means for translingual kid literature and caregiver literacies, thinking about the power of language to carry stories across generations and contexts.

*Nourishing Caregiver Collaborations* inspires conversations on what teacher preparation can look like and the implication on teacher residency programs and ethnic studies. Do our coursework and school site projects for preservice teachers include caregiver collaborations? Nawal's book lays the foundation for culturally and linguistically affirming pedagogies that center collective support.

As the book closes, the kilim emerges as a powerful metaphor woven into the narrative to symbolize the complexity of our stories *and* for the instances where we must actively resist dominant narratives that have not served us. Amidst these complexities, the book also inspires practical applications for learning spaces. It presents text recommendations, life examples, reflection questions, and anchor charts that teachers and caregivers can use. Nawal's words are a repertoire of shared experiences, offering a connection between generations and a roadmap for educators.

These reflections and explorations underscore Nawal's words as a spark for action. It compels us to honor various voices, experiences, and narratives shaping education, propelling us toward a future enriched with learning, empathy, and collaboration.

Dr. Luz Yadira Herrera
School of Education
California State University, Channel Islands

Dr. Carla España
Department of Puerto Rican and Latino Studies
Brooklyn College, City University of New York

Name _____ Title _____ Date _____

# Appendix A: See/Notice/Wonder Art Analysis Chart

|  |  | (?) |
|---|---|---|
| **What do you see?** | **What do you notice?** | **What do you wonder?** |
| | | |

# Appendix B: Synthesizing the Collective Care Framework

| Guiding Principle | Where is your school in alignment with these principles? What could be enhanced? What adjustment in practice and environment might be worth considering? |
| --- | --- |
| Academic and Joyful | |
| Culturally Nourishing | |
| Language-Inclusive | |
| Intergenerational | |
| Expansive Understanding of Literacy | |
| Consideration of Caregivers' Potentially Negative Education Experiences | |
| Neighborhood-Specific | |
| Cocreated with Caregivers | |
| Round-Reach Mentality | |

# Professional Bibliography

Afterschool Alliance. "This Is Afterschool." http://afterschoolalliance.org /documents/This-is-Afterschool-National-One-Pager.pdf.

Ahmed, Sara K. Speech at the Wisconsin Reading Association Conference, Milwaukee, WI, February 10, 2023.

Akbar, Kaveh. From a Poetry Foundation professional learning session with the author, recorded June 2022.

Alyan, Hala. "House Saints." Poetry Foundation. https://www. poetryfoundation.org/poetrymagazine/issue/151725/january-2020

Baker-Bell, April. *Linguistic Justice: Black Language, Literacy, Identity, and Pedagogy.* New York: Routledge Taylor and Francis Group, 2020.

Brown, Adrienne Marie. *Pleasure Activism.* Chico, CA: AK Press, 2019.

Buchanan-Rivera, Erica. *Identity-Affirming Classrooms: Spaces That Center Humanity.* New York: Routledge Taylor and Francis Group, 2022.

Burkins, Jan, and Kari Yates. *Shifting the Balance: 6 Ways to Bring the Science of Reading into the Balanced Literacy Classroom.* Portsmouth, NH: Stenhouse, 2021.

Chavez, Felicia Rose. *The Anti-Racist Writing Workshop.* Chicago: Haymarket Books, 2021.

Cioè-Peña, María. *(M)othering Labeled Children: Bilingualism and Disability in the Lives of Latinx Mothers.* Bristol, England: Multilingual Matters, 2021.

Coppola, Shawna. *Writing, Redefined: Broadening Our Ideas of What It Means to Compose.* Portsmouth, NH: Stenhouse, 2019.

Cruz, Colleen. *Risk Fail Rise: A Teacher's Guide to Learning from Mistakes.* Portsmouth, NH: Heinemann, 2020.

Eberhardt, Jennifer L. *Biased: Uncovering the Hidden Prejudice That Shapes What We See, Think, and Do.* New York: Viking, 2019.

Flores, Nelson, and Jonathan Rosa. "Undoing Appropriateness: Raciolinguistic Ideologies and Language Diversity in Education." *Harvard Educational Review* 85 (2015).

Garbes, Angela. *Essential Labor: Mothering as Social Change.* New York: Harper Wave, 2022.

Germán, Lorena Escoto. *Textured Teaching: A Framework for Culturally Sustaining Practices.* Portsmouth, NH: Heinemann, 2021.

González, Norma, Luis C. Moll, and Cathy Amanti, eds. *Funds of Knowledge: Theorizing Practices in Households.* New York: Routledge, 2005.

Goodall, Janet, and Caroline Montgomery. "Parental Involvement to Parental Engagement: a Continuum." *Educational Review* 66 (2013): 1–12. doi: 10.1080/00131911.2013.781576.

Gyasi, Yaa. *Transcendent Kingdom.* New York: Penguin Random House, 2020.

Haddix, Marcelle, and Yolanda Sealey-Ruiz. "Cultivating Digital and Popular Literacies as Empowering and Emancipatory Acts Among Urban Youth." *Journal of Adolescent & Adult Literacy* 56 (2012): 10.1002/JAAL.00126.

Hammond, Zaretta. *Culturally Responsive Teaching and the Brain.* Thousand Oaks, CA: Corwin, 2014.

Hawthorne, Britt, and Natasha Yglesias. *Raising Anti-Racist Children: A Practical Guide to Parenting.* New York: S&S/Simon Element, 2022.

Herrera, Luz Yadira, and Carla España. *En Comunidad: Lessons for Centering the Voices and Experiences of Bilingual Latinx Students.* Portsmouth, NH: Heinemann, 2020.

Jones, Angel. *Street Scholar: Using Public Scholarship to Educate, Advocate, and Liberate (Hip-Hop Education).* New York: Peter Lang, 2022.

Kaba, Mariame. *We Do This 'Til We Free Us: Abolitionist Organizing and Transforming Justice.* Chicago: Haymarket, 2021.

Kelly, Robin D. G. *Freedom Dreams: The Black Radical Imagination.* Boston: Beacon Press, 2003.

Kim, Jung, and Betina Hsieh. *The Racialized Experiences of Asian American Teachers in the US: Applications of Asian Critical Race Theory to Resist Marginalization.* New York: Routledge, 2022.

Kimmerer, Robin Wall. *Braiding Sweetgrass.* Minneapolis: Milkweed Editions, 2013.

Kirkland, David. "Rewriting School." *Journal of Teaching of Writing* 21, nos. 1 and 2 (2021): 83–96.

Ladson-Billings, Gloria. *Culturally Relevant Pedagogy: Asking a Different Question.* New York: Teachers College Press, 2021.

Lawrence, K., R. Campbell, and D. Skuse. "Age, Gender, and Puberty Influence the Development of Facial Emotion Recognition." *Frontiers in Psychology* 6 (2015): 761. doi: 10.3389/fpsyg.2015.00761

Mapp, Karen L., and Paul J. Kuttner. "Education in a Dual Capacity-Building Framework for Family–School Partnerships." Washington, DC: SEDL, 2013.

Meissner, Shelbi Nahwilet. "Teaching Reciprocity: Gifting and Land-Based Ethics in Indigenous Philosophy." *Teaching Ethics* 22, no. 1 (Spring 2022): 17–37. https://doi.org/10.5840/tej2022221118.

Minor, Cornelius. *We Got This: Equity, Access, and the Quest to Be Who Our Students Need Us to Be.* Portsmouth, NH: Heinemann, 2019.

Moll, Luis C., Cathy Amanti, Deborah Neff, and Norma Gonzalez. "Funds of Knowledge for Teaching: Using a Qualitative Approach to Connect Homes and Classrooms." *Theory into Practice* 31, no. 2 (1992): 132–41. http://www.jstor.com/stable/1476399.

Muhammad, Gholdy. *Cultivating Genius: An Equity Framework for Culturally and Historically Responsive Literacy.* New York: Scholastic, 2020.

———. *Unearthing Joy: A Guide to Culturally and Historically Responsive Curriculum and Instruction.* New York: Scholastic, 2023.

Nava, Pedro E. "Abuelita Storytelling: From Pain to Possibility and Implications for Higher Education." *Storytelling, Self, Society* 13, no. 2 (Fall 2017): 151–69. https://www.jstor.org/stable/10.13110/storselfsoci.13.2.0151.

Nichols, Maria. *Building Bigger Ideas: A Process for Teaching Purposeful Talk.* Portsmouth, NH: Heinemann, 2019.

Nieto, Sonia. "Moving Beyond Tolerance in Multicultural Education." *Multicultural Education*, 1, no. 4 (Spring 1994): 9–12, 35–38.

Okun, Tema. "White Supremacy Culture." https://www.whitesupremacyculture .info/.

——. White Supremacy Culture." dRWorks, 1999.

Richards, Akilah S. *Raising Free People: Unschooling as Liberation and Healing Work*. Oakland, CA: PM Press, 2020.

Salesses, Matthew. *Craft in the Real World: Rethinking Fiction Writing and Workshopping*. New York: Penguin Random House, 2021.

San Pedro, Timothy. *Protecting the Promise: Indigenous Education Between Mothers and Their Children* (Culturally Sustaining Pedagogies Series), edited by Django Paris. New York: Teachers College, 2021.

Shalaby, Carla. *Troublemakers: Lessons in Freedom from Young Children at School*. New York: The New Press, 2017.

Smith, Clint. "Tradition." *Above Ground*. New York: Little, Brown and Company, 2023.

Smith, Emily Esfahani. *The Power of Meaning: Crafting a Life That Matters*. New York: Penguin Random House, 2017.

Suárez-Orozco, Carola, Marcelo M. Suárez-Orozco, and Irina Todorova. *Learning a New Land: Immigrant Students in American Society*. Cambridge, MA: Belknap Press, 2010.

Tahir, Sabaa. *All My Rage: A Novel*. New York: Razorbill, 2022.

Tatum, Alfred. *Reading for Their Life: (Re)Building the Textual Lineages of African American Adolescent Males*. First Edition. Portsmouth, NH: Heinemann, 2009.

Teng, C. L., C. J. Ng, H. Nik-Sherina, A. H. Zilinawait, and S. F. Ton. "The Accuracy of Mother's Touch to Detect Fever in Children: A Systematic Review." *Journal of Tropical Pediatrics* 54, no. 1 (2008): 70–73. doi: 10.1093 /tropej/fmm077.

Turkle, Sherry. *Reclaiming Conversation: The Power of Talk in a Digital Age*. New York: Penguin Random House, 2016.

Valenzuela, Angela. *Subtractive Schooling: U.S.-Mexican Youth and the Politics of Caring*. Albany: SUNY Press, 1999.

Vogel, Sara, and Ofelia García. "Translanguaging." In *Oxford Research Encyclopedia, Education*, 2017. https://academicworks.cuny.edu/cgi /viewcontent.cgi?article=1448&context=gc_pubs

Vu, Don. *Life, Literacy and the Pursuit of Happiness: Supporting Our Immigrant and Refugee Children Through the Power of Reading*. New York: Scholastic, 2021.

# Index